BENJAMIN FRANKLIN

"Au Genie de Franklin," by Jean Honoré Fragonard (1732–1806). *(The Metropolitan Museum of Art, Gift of William H. Huntington, 1882)*

BENJAMIN FRANKLIN

Statesman-Philosopher or Materialist?

Edited by WILBUR R. JACOBS
University of California, Santa Barbara

HOLT, RINEHART AND WINSTON
New York • Chicago • San Francisco • Atlanta
Dallas • Montreal • Toronto • London • Sydney

Cover illustration: Benjamin Franklin as a fireman, from a painting by a mid-nineteenth-century artist. "America's first fireman" is seen in a nineteenth-century work hat with the shield of the Union Fire Company, the band of volunteers organized by Franklin in 1736. *(Insurance Company of North America)*

CONTENTS

CHRONOLOGY

1706   Born in Boston, January 17

1714   Spends year in Boston Grammar School

1716–18   Assists father, Josiah, a candlemaker

1718–23   Becomes apprentice to his half-brother James; assists James in publishing *New England Courant* (1722–23), and prints his *Dogood Papers* anonymously in the newspaper (1722)

1723–24   Runs away from brother, breaking indenture; travels to New York and later to Philadelphia, where he is employed by the printer, Samuel Keimer

1724–26   Leaves for London, where he is employed in printing houses and where he publishes *A Dissertation on Liberty and Necessity, Pleasure and Pain* (1725). Returning to America, he writes *Journal of a Voyage from London to Philadelphia* (1726)

1726–41   Forms Junto Club (1727); buys Keimer's newspaper and publishes it as *The Pennsylvania Gazette* (1729); becomes Public Printer for Pennsylvania Assembly (1730); founds a subscription library, The Library Company of Philadelphia (1731); begins *Poor Richard's Almanack* (1732); establishes Union Fire Company in Philadelphia (1736); becomes Philadelphia postmaster and is elected to Assembly (1737); begins publication of *The General Magazine and Historical Chronicle* (1741)

1742–51   Invents Franklin stove (1742); establishes American Philosophical Society (1744); writes *Reflections on Courtship and Marriage* (1746); retires from business (1748); *Experiments and Observations on Electricity, Made at Philadelphia in America by Mr. Franklin* (1751) is published under the sponsorship of Peter Collinson

1752–63   Collinson's edition of Franklin's works (including kite experiment) is translated into French (1752); represents Pennsylvania as Indian Commissioner at Carlisle treaty (1753); proposes plan for intercolonial union at Albany Conference (1754); appointed colonial agent for Pennsylvania in England (1757); prints *The Way to Wealth* (1758); tours Holland and Belgium (1761); tours colonies to inspect post offices (1763)

1764–70   Represents Pennsylvania as agent in London (1764); gives Lord Grenville Pennsylvania resolution against Stamp Act (1765); is questioned in House of Commons on Stamp tax (1766); visits France and meets French Physiocrats (1767); is appointed agent for Massachusetts (1770)

1771–76   Begins *Autobiography* (1771); is elected to Royal Academy of Sciences, Paris; is questioned before Privy Council on Hutchinson-Oliver letters (1774); returns to America (1775); presides at Pennsylvania Constitutional Convention (1776); as American representative leaves for Paris, December 31, 1776

1777–90   Signs treaty for mutual defense with France (1778); signs Treaty of Paris with John Adams and John Jay, ending the War of Independence (1783); signs treaty of friendship with Prussia (1785); elected president of the Pennsylvania Society for the Abolition of Slavery, and is Pennsylvania delegate to the Constitutional Convention (1787); continues writing *Autobiography* (1788); dies in Philadelphia, April 17, 1790

INTRODUCTION

Benjamin Franklin was a man of extraordinary talents and skills. His mark is on practically every science and profession known to society in eighteenth-century America. Highly respected as statesman and scientist, he gained fame also as a writer, inventor, diplomat, moralist, thinker, and philanthropist. As a man he was reasonable, intelligent, and personable—bound to be a great favorite among those who write about the American past. The wide scale of his talents, however, has not earned him complete approval in our age. Some of the critics have questioned his sincerity and have regarded his many abilities with suspicion, feeling perhaps that such remarkable versatility should not be taken seriously. Franklin's life and writings have actually engendered considerable animosity, and he has been the subject of emotional verbal battles between his admirers and his critics. If these battles had been confined to Franklin the man, they might have been less heated. But less obvious and submerged issues have generated much of the warmth.

One question that has been hotly debated is whether Franklin, a man who was relatively unconcerned with the theoretical aspects of religion and philosophy and almost indifferent to the literary and artistic achievements of his age, deserves to be regarded as a great figure of the eighteenth century. A second question is related to the first: To what extent was Franklin the first "typical" American? This practical rather than contemplative man, this ambitious, diligent and not overly subtle man, is frequently considered partially responsible for the direction in which the American character has developed.

Franklin's tremendously popular *Autobiography* in many respects exemplifies the American national character, and for this reason much of the comment on Franklin is conditioned by the observer's particular attitude toward modern America. Those who approve of the American tradition of common sense, practicality, and self-sufficiency admire Franklin. Those who are dismayed by the intellectual and moral limitations of the practical outlook on life find little in him to praise. As these two contrasting views tend to polarize, enthusiasts and critics tend to place Franklin in the category of hero or villain.

Another matter that has been contested with some heat is Franklin's political posture, whether he was conservative or revolutionary. This question is,

1

of course, closely related to the larger debate on whether the American Revolution was a *real* revolution of the American people.

Much of the literature on Franklin, then, if not of a controversial nature, is at least colored by the firm viewpoints of the various writers. In many respects, however, it is hard to imagine a man less likely to arouse antagonism, for he appears to have been well-adjusted, honest, straightforward, and easy to understand. Born in Boston in 1706, the tenth son of Josiah Franklin, an English immigrant who made a living as a tallow chandler and soap-boiler, young Benjamin first worked in his father's shop. At the age of twelve, he was apprenticed to James, an older half-brother who was a printer. In 1721 James had begun printing the *New England Courant,* one of Boston's first newspapers. Following a series of disagreements with his brother, Franklin in 1723 ran off to Philadelphia, where he was fortunate to find work in a printing house.

In Philadelphia, Franklin made a new life for himself. As a young man he adopted frugal eating habits and allowed himself ample fresh air and exercise (he became an expert swimmer) in what became a lifelong effort to preserve good health. In 1730, the year of his marriage to Deborah Read, he established his own printing house and published *The Pennsylvania Gazette.* In the following decades while serving as a Pennsylvania Assemblyman, he allowed time for a series of investigations that led to his invention of the Franklin stove and his electrical experiments. By the time he accepted the post of colonial agent (representing Pennsylvania and other colonies in London) in the 1760s, the scientific academies of the great nations of Europe had elected him to membership as an eminent scientist.

In the later years of his life Franklin served his country as a statesman and diplomat. His experience as a colonial agent gave him knowledge of international politics and enabled him to gain French support for American independence. In 1783 he participated in the final negotiations of the Treaty of Paris—a treaty that recognized the sovereignty of the new American nation. At eighty-two, in his sturdy old age, Franklin was still active enough to play a significant role at the Constitutional Convention.

Even before Franklin died, on April 17, 1790, there were conflicting accounts of his importance, A coterie of contemporary critics, including John Adams, had reservations about his sincerity and competence. In the nineteenth century, however, historians such as Jared Sparks, who edited Franklin's papers, were convinced that he was a statesman and diplomat of high stature. Later historians and creative writers were irritated by his emphasis on materialistic practicality, and portrayed him as a grasping individual with a hunger for fame and fortune.

The majority of scholars and readers, however, have seen little reason to criticize Franklin. He has mainly been admired for his practical energy and for the tremendous impetus he gave to improving the society of his age. Besides, he was a statesman of considerable eminence who preached and often practiced a morality emphasizing honesty, industry, thrift, and solicitude for one's neighbors and society at large. There are few among us who strenuously object to such an outlook on life.

In reading these essays, one might ask to what extent Franklin deserves a reputation as a typical American money-grubbing materialist? Or does he, on the other hand, actually mirror the best side of American civilization? Carl Van Doren, author of the most highly regarded biography of Franklin and of the opening essay printed here, is convinced of the high order of his accomplishments. Van Doren seems to go further than the majority of Franklin admirers when he sets his hero on a towering pedestal, above other statesmen of the Revolutionary age, describing him as a "genius," "a very great man," with a "supreme mind." Even friendly commentators might find such comments a bit strong. Van Doren argues that Franklin was truly eminent in a variety of fields of achievement and was such an original thinker that he would have been recognized for his greatness in any age. Franklin's "superiority," Van Doren maintains, is difficult to measure because he moved from task to task with what appears to be complete ease. "Mind and will, talent and art, strength and ease, wit and grace met in him as if nature had been lavish and happy when he was shaped." According to Van Doren, Franklin's *Autobiography* is deceptive because it makes him appear more ordinary than he really was.

No other writer represented in the essays printed here is so enthusiastic in his admiration of Franklin. On more than one occasion Van Doren's praise seems overdone: "It has recently been more than once remarked—and printed — that Benjamin Franklin was the American Leonardo da Vinci. This is American modesty, if not colonialism. Why not occasionally say that Leonardo da Vinci was the Italian Benjamin Franklin?" Why not join Van Doren in putting forth such rhetorical praise with nationalistic overtones? Van Doren's purpose here, it seems, is to claim for Franklin a supreme, elevated position in history that even Franklin himself might not have wholly accepted. Or one might argue that in Van Doren the sly Benjamin Franklin found at last the biographer who would give him enduring fame. Indeed, there is evidence to show that a motivating force in Franklin's life was to build himself "a monument" by governing his behavior by the rule "Imitate Jesus and Socrates." Van Doren perhaps wrote exactly the kind of biography that the shrewd Franklin wanted him to write.

The opposing view of Franklin, however, is not easily put aside. Among the most spirited and outspoken of Franklin's critics is the English novelist, literary critic, and poet D. H. Lawrence. In an eloquent critique of Franklin, wicked and witty and fun to read, Lawrence chips away at the heroic image:

"Why should the snuff-colored little trap have wanted to take us all in? Why did he do it? Out of sheer human cussedness"; "cunning little Benjamin"; the "dummy American." Lawrence's hostility toward Franklin tends to give his essay a somewhat emotional tone. In mentioning Franklin's achievements, Lawrence ignores some of the most significant ones (his role in founding the Academy of Philadelphia, for instance) and stresses those that might be ridiculed: "He swept and lighted the streets of young Philadelphia." Lawrence's technique in describing Franklin's scientific achievements is to state that "He invented electrical appliances." Van Doren, by contrast, gives this warm praise: "What he called his 'conjectures and suppositions' about electricity make up the Principia of the science."

Lawrence, who was himself almost indifferent to material success, found in Franklin a model of the values he destested. Those who are familiar with Lawrence's poetry and novels will nct be surprised by the sharpness of his attack. Franklin's stress on reason and moderation and his idea that sexual indulgence should be sanctioned only for reasons of health and offspring angered Lawrence, who believed that impulses and feelings really sway human actions. Lawrence focuses his indignation on the word "venery" used by Franklin. This one word becomes a symbol of Franklin's materialism. Can we say that Lawrence's criticisms are unjustified? Does his spectrum of evidence cover a wider range of thought than Van Doren's? It is not easy to deal with such questions because Lawrence's technique of argumentation involves Lawrence himself as well as Franklin the man.

In the second section, which evaluates Franklin as apostle of the modern age, we are less concerned with his attitudes and character (although these are not overlooked) than with his political, social, and scientific ideas and work. Vernon Louis Parrington, a progressive in his own time, sees a parallel between Daniel Defoe and Franklin in that both used their pens as weapons to improve their societies. Whereas Defoe was in England, however, Franklin by accident of birth lived in America where he was more successful in bringing about changes for the betterment of the common man. Parrington views Franklin as a man receptive to new concepts and free of the prejudices of his own class and time: here is a statesman-philosopher who is generations ahead of his contemporaries, a man who rejected mercantilism in favor of free trade; similarly, he adopted the concept that labor is the measure of value generations before it was generally accepted. For the admirer of Franklin, Parrington's assessment is penetrating and full. Franklin, Parrington argues, "does not reveal the full measure of human aspiration." But he concludes with an astute estimate of Franklin's greatness: "In his modesty, his willingness to compromise, his openmindedness, his clear and luminous understanding, his charity—above all, in his desire to subdue the ugly facts of society to some more rational scheme of things—he proved himself a great and useful man, one of the greatest and most useful whom America has produced."

Although Parrington regards Franklin as an eighteenth-century sociologist, I. Bernard Cohen maintains that Franklin was a distinguished scientist whose reputation has suffered because those appraising his work have not been properly qualified to undertake the task. Historians, for the most part, have been poorly equipped to deal with Franklin's scientific achievements, and scientists writing about Franklin have been untrained in historical background, in techniques of writing, and in knowledge of eighteenth-century science. Unfortunately, writers not well versed in the history of science have emphasized Franklin's practical inventions and neglected his scientific thought. Judged by the standards of the eighteenth century, Franklin was nevertheless a scientist of first rank whose "fame and public renown as a scientist," Cohen argues, "was in no small measure responsible for his success in international statesmanship." Cohen argues further that Franklin's contribution to pure science, especially in physics, has been downgraded because modern science has been largely built upon achievements of nineteenth-century European scientists. American scientists have looked to their European masters; they have not understood the direct line of advance going back to Franklin and early American history.

Franklin's political coloration, too, has not always been properly evaluated, according to Bernhard Knollenberg, author of the third essay in this group. Knollenberg launches his argument by stating that Franklin was a "philosophical revolutionist" rather than a political conservative. Franklin questioned established religious doctrines; he opposed the proprietors in Pennsylvania in their efforts to make their lands exempt from taxation; opposed Parliament in its attempt to levy internal colonial taxes, and he originated new revolutionary scientific theories—these facts are cited as evidence of Franklin's revolutionary stand.

Yet are we really convinced that Franklin was a revolutionary, or that he qualified even as a "philosophical revolutionist," to use Knollenberg's watered down term? One has the impression that the author of this provocative article would be happier with a more fiery Franklin to fit his theme. Nevertheless, Knollenberg makes the point that an open-minded, intelligent Franklin, a man with a skeptical questioning mind, gave strong support to the Revolutionary movement and did not hesitate to identify himself with its leadership.

David Levin, author of the last essay in this group, also believes that Franklin's image has been distorted. He does not see Franklin as a revolutionary, however, but rather as an immensely talented man who deliberately gave the world a special image of himself in his *Autobiography*. Franklin portrayed himself, Levin maintains, as a representative of his age and country. There is an intentional oversimplification in the book, for Franklin's purpose was to help youth to avoid danger in the open competitive world and to point the way toward success. Thus in his *Autobiography* Franklin left out much that did not conform to his plan of writing, as, for instance, his life in the fashionable society of his day and his fascination with certain French women who competed for his favors. Instead, Franklin sketched a story of his life, with a view to demonstrating that thrift, work, and self-education could prepare a person for later public service and scientific pursuits. Franklin, like other autobiographers, *"actually creates himself as a character."*

The third section of this volume is primarily concerned with Franklin as the pragmatic businessman, the activist who gets things done. The essays in this group move closer to the Franklin image of *Poor Richard's Almanac*, so it is not unexpected that the critical spirit is especially strong here. Charles Augustin Sainte-Beuve, a Frenchman, pinpoints Franklin's lack of romantic feeling in relations with women, his "reasonable" attitude toward romance. Is Sainte-Beuve in error in arguing that one must not ask Franklin to appreciate the bloom of chivalry or even to adopt a religion that does not have utility? In his analysis Sainte-Beuve argues that Franklin lacked enthusiasm, devotion, passionate feeling, and sentiment. On the positive side, Sainte-Beuve finds a judicious combination of wit, common sense, and integrity. Although Franklin sometimes used poetic expressions, he was surely no poet.

Charles Angoff, dwells on the point that Franklin lacked poetic sensibilities. Franklin gave no impetus to a school of literature. He wrote nothing that could be called great, and although he wrote with clarity, he had little to say of real significance. He had no originality of thought, but like a sponge absorbed the ideas of the age of rationalism that were then current. He was muddled, confused, and inconsistent, and was an opportunist in thought and action. Franklin was, in short, according to Angoff, a lowbrow who spread vulgarity over the land. Franklin's seeming indifference to spiritual things prompts Angoff to severe condemnation: "He extolled the virtues of honesty, industry, chastity, cleanliness, and temperance—all excellent things. But it never occurred to him that with these alone life is not worth a fool's second thought. Philosophy, poetry, and the arts spring from different sources."

Harsh judgments of this kind are easy to make, but do they actually bear up under scrutiny of the facts? Franklin is elusive to the critic. It is not enough to read his main works. A shortcoming in one will be compensated for in another. If one criticizes a particular point, one may find years later that the criticism is met in a letter, possibly a previously unpublished letter.

Franklin is likely to appeal to many modern Americans precisely because he was a moralist and practical man of affairs. Most modern audiences would approve of his detached attitude toward religion. Would segments of modern youth agree with Angoff's complaint that Franklin lacked grandeur of soul, a feeling for noble, abstract, and philosophical ideals? Would such youthful critics agree that Angoff's criticism is based upon judgment of Franklin as a writer, and writing was only a by-product of his other activities? Is it damning, as Angoff argues, that such a man wrote nothing that was actually great?

Turning from Angoff's censures of Franklin to Philip Gleason's searching essay, the reader can examine eighteenth-century attitudes toward Franklin, many of which differ from those of today. Gleason places his spotlight on the Pennsylvania assembly election of 1764, in which upper-class Philadelphians regarded the candidate Franklin with distaste. Franklin's political enemies appear to have classified him as an untrustworthy scoundrel, an opportunist without personal morals. Yet, interestingly enough, there were no contemporary complaints about his materialistic moralizing about thrift and practicality.

Gleason's scholarly detachment contrasts with the approach in the essay by the poet William Carlos Williams. Like D. H. Lawrence, Williams is dismayed by Franklin, a smug, practical, unpoetic figure who "played with lightning and the French court." He notes that Franklin had a sinister influence upon the development of America; he is the symbol of our niggardliness and sluggishness, which resulted in our hoarding wealth and building walls against the wilderness. Williams thinks that American stupidity in not appreciating the grandeur of the wilderness and the nobility of the Indian can be traced to Franklin's strong influence upon the growth of our national character. Was Franklin the materialist in part responsible for the American exploitation of the Indian and the wilderness? A further question here (though not developed by Williams): What about America's looting and misuse of the land and modern ecological problems? Is a figure like Franklin a symbol of such crass materialism?

F. L. Lucas compares Franklin with other eighteenth-century literary figures. Despite his focus on Franklin as a writer, he shows that he truly *likes* Franklin. He praises his intelligence, wisdom, honesty, and devotion to the service of mankind. Lucas sees the thread of pragmatism in Franklin's life as an asset that gave him deserved fame in his lifetime and even today. The world could afford fewer Lawrences, Lucas concludes, but it could do with many more Franklins.

The final two essays in this volume deal primarily with Franklin as the prototype of the American. Esmond Wright maintains that the self-made Franklin was the father of all Yankees. A printer, trader, and empirical observer of society and life, he was a man of worldly wisdom, at home in England and France as well as in America. He believed in free men, free speech, and free trade. Not so flatteringly, Wright mentions Franklin's wealth and identifies *Poor Richard* as an early syndicated column in American journalism.

Wright's article helps to clarify certain misconceptions about Franklin that are rooted in the eighteenth-century preoccupation with reputation and success. Franklin's self-discipline, moralizing, and character training are related to eighteenth-century ideals of self-control, reason, and balance. Thus Franklin's readiness to give advice in his own time did not bring forth the negative reaction it does today. Does Wright help us to understand changing standards of values and the tentative nature of historical judgments?

The concluding essay by John William Ward pinpoints the problem of describing Franklin's character: Franklin assumed many guises, and at times whatever stance was convenient. He preached hard work, but retired from his printshop at forty-two. He advocated prudence and caution, yet he joined, and indeed became a leader in, a revolutionary movement. He looked after his own personal advancement, but most of his adult life was devoted to serving others. Franklin played the role that suited the circumstances. In his early Philadelphia years he wore the mask of humility, and in France he played the part of cavalier, sometimes lapsing into the role of a backwoods democrat. Franklin's good humor, his self-awareness (in his *Autobiography*) show us, according to Ward, that he believed in the importance of appearance. His common-sense utilitarianism made him value the expectations of those around him. The remarkable rise of Franklin in society resembles much of the American national character. He symbolizes, according to Ward, the rapid social flux in our society and the question of identity that persists among Americans: "Who am I?" In this sense, Franklin is an archetype in our history.

As the selections in this volume make clear, Franklin's life and work have a particular but complex relation to the development of modern America. Can one agree that it is difficult to accept him completely despite his accomplishments and obvious virtues? Some writers represented in this volume cannot accept him at all, and others have pointed reservations. Is it not true that Franklin's significance today stems from all the conflicting feelings he arouses within us? Does not reading about Franklin force us to reexamine the moral, the practical and the philosophical ideals upon which American society is based? And finally, are his career and the example of his life part of the mainstream of the American national experience?

In the reprinted selections footnotes appearing in the original sources have in general been omitted unless they contribute to the argument or better understanding of the selection.

CONFLICTING VIEWS

"He was father of all the Yankees. . . . His worldly wisdom was suited to the *philosophes* in Paris and in Edinburgh; it was suited, too, to the old wives in the chimney corner, summing up a lifetime of neighbourly experience."—Esmond Wright.

"Thrift, industry, and determination were essential virtues in the building of a nation, but they were not, then or at any other time in history, of sufficient human dignity to build a life philosophy on. . . . The vulgarity he spread is still with us."—Charles Angoff.

"A wit and philosopher, rich in learning, charming in manners, ripe in the wisdom of this world, resourceful in dealing with men and events, he was one of the most delightful as he was one of the greatest men produced by the English race in the eighteenth century."—Vernon Louis Parrington.

"Oh, Franklin was the first downright American. He knew what he was about, the sharp little man. He set up the first dummy American."—D. H. Lawrence.

"We admire, I think, the lusty good sense of the man who triumphs in the world that he accepts, yet at the same time we are uneasy with the man who wears so many masks that we are never sure who is there behind them."—John William Ward.

"He is our wise prophet of chicanery, the great buffoon, the face on the penny stamp."—William Carlos Williams.

"Franklin was the earliest American whom, without limiting ourselves to national terms, we can call a very great man. . . . Franklin's eminence was in his almost supreme mind that moved to its countless tasks with what seems perfect ease."—Carl Van Doren.

CARL VAN DOREN (1885–1950), literary editor and writer, is author of the most distinguished biography of Franklin. He contends, in what was originally an address, that Franklin was certainly one of the greatest of men. Franklin's "almost supreme mind" helps to explain his genius. One should not be misled by the homespun picture of himself that Franklin retouched for his *Autobiography*. Franklin himself is so remarkable that no one could have invented such a figure. His personality, according to Van Doren, was much like that of "a harmonious multitude." How does Van Doren deal with the vexing question of Franklin's vanity?*

Carl Van Doren

"A Very Great Man"

Franklin had, I think, the most eminent mind that has ever existed in America. No wonder there are so many legendary misconceptions of him that it is difficult now to restore and comprehend him in the great integrity of his mind, character, and personality. He appears, somehow, to be a syndicate of men. We study him as a scientist, as a diplomat, as a statesman, as a businessman, as an economist, as a printer, as a humorist and wit, as a great writer, as a sage, and as a landmark in the history of human speech about the common ways of life. What had been said before he so often said better. He was great in friendship, and in his later years was probably the most renowned private citizen on earth. It has recently been more than once remarked —and printed—that Benjamin Franklin was the American Leonardo di Vinci. This is American modesty, if not colonialism. Why not occasionally say that Leonardo di Vinci was the Italian Benjamin Franklin?

Franklin was the earliest American whom, without limiting ourselves to national terms, we can call a very great man. When you try to define his particular greatness you run into what John Adams felt in his jealous days in Paris. Adams was a great man, but not a very great man. A great man such as Adams living with a very great man such as Franklin cannot tell the difference between himself and the other. Adams

*From Carl Van Doren, "Meet Dr. Franklin," in The Franklin Institute, *Meet Dr. Franklin* (Philadelphia, 1943), pp. 1–10.

could not tell why people thought the difference to be so enormous. Nor can anybody express the difference better than with a fairly common, if not entirely just, geographical analogy. Imagine yourself in a range of mountains. You look up, and several of the mountains seem to you, from where you stand, as high as the master of them all. But when you get to a distance which gives perspective you see that the great mountain towers above the others, which are, in a sense, only foothills to it. This was true of many men with whom Franklin was associated during his life, who were as far from being aware of his genuine superiority as posterity has sometimes been since then. Moreover, his superiority is the hardest kind to measure. We can sometimes measure superiority when it shows itself in outward acts, achievements, tumults, benefits, or damages. Franklin's eminence was in his almost supreme mind that moved to its countless tasks with what seems perfect ease. Both the supremacy and the ease are hard for us to explain because they are so nearly unique in history that comparisons fail us. And without comparisons there can be no measurements.

There are, of course, people who take an attitude toward Franklin that may remind us of the fate of Aristides. For his virtues, you will remember, he had a peevish vote cast against him by an illiterate man who was tired of hearing Aristides called Aristides the Just. We often have an impulse to fear and distrust great excellence. We say we like it, but in our hearts we suspect it of being more—and consequently less—than human. When we say this or that hero is "human" we always mean he is weak in some way that is comforting. All of us are weak, and we like to believe this is human of us. When we find a similar

weakness in a great man we are pleased because it means that the great are not so much greater than we are after all.

It is now and then asked if Franklin did not get most or many of his ideas from other men, and then out of vanity take the credit to himself. I do not think Franklin was particularly vain. In the third paragraph of his Autobiography he disarmingly admitted that telling his story might gratify his vanity. "Most people dislike vanity in others, whatever share they have of it themselves; but I give it quarter wherever I meet with it, being persuaded that it is often productive of good to its possessor, and to others that are within his sphere of action; and therefore, in many cases, it would not be altogether absurd if a man were to thank God for his vanity among the other comforts of life." Franklin knew that the false modesty which men conventionally affect is a mode of self-conscious egotism.

What could Franklin do when he wrote his Autobiography but tell of things he had done or helped do? Why should he have talked as with his hand over his mouth or his elbow over his head? Everybody knew he was great and famous. For him to pretend not to know that would have been silly, a form of stage fright. In a letter about the classic epigram of Turgot which said Franklin had snatched the lightning from the sky and the scepter from tyrants, Franklin in 1781 honestly protested. "It ascribes too much to me, especially in what relates to the tyrant; the Revolution having been the work of many able and brave men, wherein it is sufficient honor for me if I am allowed a small share."

Or go back to an earlier year in Franklin's life, when he was not so famous and might have been tempted not to be so generous. In the fall of 1753 he got together what he called a "philosophical packet" of letters exchanged between him and various scientific friends of his in America. It was an important year for Franklin. The king of France had complimented the remote Philadelphia tradesman on his electrical discoveries, Harvard and Yale had given him honorary degrees, the Royal Society in November awarded him the Copley gold medal. The "philosophical packet" was to signalize what Franklin hoped would be a fresh beginning for him in the scientific career he looked forward to. Among these papers was a letter from James Bowdoin of Boston, dated November 12, in which he—before any other scientist so far as is known—hit on the first true explanation of "luminosity" (phosphorescence) in sea water: "that the said appearance might be caused by a great number of little animals, floating on the surface of the sea, which, on being disturbed, might, by expanding their finns, or otherwise moving themselves, expose such a part of their bodies as exhibits a luminous appearance, somewhat in the manner of a glowworm, or fire-fly."

Here was a subject Franklin had already speculated on. He had at first conjectured that this luminosity was "owing to electric fire, produced by friction between the particles of water and those of salt. Living far from the sea, I had then no opportunity of making experiments on the sea water, and so embraced this opinion too hastily. For in 1750 and 1751, being occasionally on the sea coast, I found, by experiments, that sea water in a bottle, though at first it would by agitation appear luminous, yet in a few hours it lost that virtue; hence, and from this . . . I first began to doubt of my former hypothesis, and to suspect that the luminous appearance in sea water must be owing to some other principles."

Bowdoin's conjecture at once struck Franklin as sounder than his own. "It is indeed very possible, " he wrote in a letter dated 13 December, "that an extremely small animalcule, too small to be visible even by the best glasses, may yet give a visible light. I remember to have taken notice, in a drop of kennel water magnified by the solar microscope to the bigness of a cart-wheel, there were numbers of visible animalcules swimming about; but I was sure there were likewise some which I could not see, even with that magnifier; for the wake they made in swimming to and fro was very visible, though the body that made it was not so. Now, if I could see the wake of an invisible animalcule, I imagine I might much more easily see its light if it were of the luminous kind. For how small is the extent of a ship's wake, compared with that of the light of her lantern."

Dr. Edwin Grant Conklin of the American Philosophical Society recently told me that a Japanese scholar had called Franklin's comment on these animalcules in sea water the earliest guess at the existence and nature of the microorganisms, as we should now call them, which are responsible for the phenomenon. Franklin had nothing to do with the error. He kept back his own letter (to be published long after his death), and sent Bowdoin's to London, where it was read before the Royal Society in December 1756 and later included in the 1769 edition of Franklin's "Experiments and Observations on Electricity," as "a Letter from J. B. Esq; in Boston, to B. F. concerning the Light in Sea-Water." The credit was Bowdoin's, and Franklin plainly gave it to him.

This same 1769 volume, among the most fascinating in the whole range of eighteenth-century "philosophical" writings, punctiliously credited Thomas

Hopkinson, Ebenezer Kinnersley, and Philip Syng with their original suggestions and discoveries made during the "Philadelphia experiments." If the three came to be overlooked in the light of their greater colleague, it was hardly Franklin's fault. Reporting to Peter Collinson in London, Franklin constantly spoke of "our electrical enquiries" and the things "we" had found out, never pretending to have done the work alone. The first collection of his "Experiments and Observations" (1751) was possibly printed in London before Franklin in Philadelphia had known it was to be. Because he alone had written the reports, his name alone was given on the titlepage. In his own copy of the pamphlet he marked each experiment with the initials of the discoverer: Hopkinson's once, Kinnersley's seven times and once jointly with Franklin's, Syng's three times. There can be little doubt that Franklin was always chief among the experimenters, as there can be none that he was the best writer among them. But he did not make excessive claims for himself. What happened was that as he went on growing more and more famous, the world credited him with more and more achievements, past as well as present. In the world at large, first men are dramatically first, and the rest nowhere to speak of.

I know it is commonly said that the Autobiography is a retouched photograph in which Franklin emphasizes his own share in the life of his times and minimizes that of other men. I also know that I have spent many days and weeks investigating this very matter and have come to the conclusion that he left out things he had done more often than he even seemed to claim to have done things he had not. Philadelphia during the great years of the Junto (1727 to 1757)

was a town of remarkable intellectual activity, and its history has not yet been truly written as I hope it will some day be. But no matter what claims may be made for other men, Franklin emerges as the chief among them, the energizing, galvanizing source of two-thirds of the town's important enterprises.

When I am told, as I occasionally am, that I make Franklin out as larger than life, I can only answer that Franklin must have been what he was, because nobody could have invented such a figure. Stranger things happen in fact than in fiction. Nature is richer in invention than men are. The great characters in fiction are almost always heroes who have each of them some ruling passion, with enough human weaknesses to give him a reasonable credibility. Romantic creation is most likely to be exaggeration along a few lines. But the more you study Franklin the more lines you find running out from him in all directions, and the more facts that no poet—however romantic and exaggerative—would ever have thought of inventing. The wonder of Franklin is the facts that are true about him. The more exact the research into his character, the more surprising the adventure.

Too much emphasis has been laid, I think, on his simple practical ingenuities. You go into a grocer's and see the clerk taking objects down from high shelves with a device based on the "long arm" which Franklin invented to get at his books. Most of us have in our kitchens a combination chair-and-stepladder which Franklin seems to have devised; and in our fireplaces a draft such as he had made for his fireplace in Craven Street. He has been credited with the invention of the rocking chair, which I believe he did not invent, though in his last years he had one which automatically fanned him when he rocked. But the ingenuity that went into these gadgets is less notable than the fundamental ideas behind Franklin's principal inventions.

If, for example, we read his remarkable pamphlet about what he called the Pennsylvanian fireplace, later known as the Franklin stove, we should not be too much taken by the salesmanlike adroitness of his arguments. It is true he was adroit, particularly in his claims that the use of the stove would be beneficial to the health, complexion, and beauty of women. Such arguments were as likely to be effective in 1744 as they would be in 1939. But Franklin believed they were sound, as they were. He had not designed his stove purely for economy in fuel. He had strongly in mind the great importance of proper ventilation, and its value for health. He even took into account an esthetic element. His stove, unlike the Dutch and German stoves of the time, allowed people to see the fire, "which is in itself a pleasant thing." In 1744 Franklin had been using his stove, he said, for "the four winters past," which takes the invention back to 1740. But he put off writing about it till he had announced the organization of the American Philosophical Society. His pamphlet was in effect his first contribution to the work of this new league of scientists. As if to give his little treatise the dignity of learning, he accompanied it with notes from various impressive sources, one of them in Latin.

Certainly the lightning rod was not a gadget. The experiment which Franklin proposed, to prove whether electricity and lightning were identical, and his own separate demonstration with the kite, must be ranked with the most fundamental as well as the most striking experiments in scientific history. The story of the kite is now so old and so familiar that it has come to seem a pleasant legend, not much more real to us than the customary pictures of the scene, which show Franklin's son as a little boy when in fact he was twenty-one or so and as tall as his father. The experiment, because it solved a mystery, has so deprived lightning of its terror that it no longer overawes men. Franklin, drawing the lightning from the skies, removed it from the dread region of mythology. Kant was not speaking for picturesque effect when he said Franklin was a new Prometheus who had stolen fire from heaven. The expression meant, literally, that Franklin had made men equals of the gods and therefore free of an ancient slavish dread. Nobody in 1752 felt that the kite story was a quaint little incident. It was something immense, and it gave Franklin the reputation of a wizard, not too much unlike Merlin or Roger Bacon —or, in our day, Einstein.

I have, I suppose, already made it clear that I do not agree with those almost unanimous modern commentators on Franklin who think of him as primarily an ingenious inventor. I will go further and say that I think his fundamental conjectures are more important than his inventions. He said of himself: "I own I have too strong a penchant to the building of hypotheses; they indulge my natural indolence." But these hypotheses were as truly original as anything he ever invented. What he called his "conjectures and suppositions" about electricity make up the Principia of the science. Nor did he confine himself to one branch of science, or to science as a whole. His notes in 1743 on the origin of northeast storms were the first step toward a scientific meteorology. In his "Observations Concerning the Increase of Mankind, Peopling of Countries, etc.," written in

1751, he not only anticipated Malthus, who acknowledged his debt to Franklin, but also forecast the theory of the American frontier later associated with the name of Frederick Jackson Turner. In 1754 Franklin in his famous letters to Governor Shirley of Massachusetts set down his far-sighted plan for equal justice to the various parts of the British Empire, and summed up almost all the American arguments of the Revolution. In 1762 he wrote the earliest piece of scientific musical criticism, and in 1768 said as much as has been said since about the need of reform in English spelling. He was the first scholar who studied the Gulf Stream (1769) and had some understanding of it and the possible use of it by navigators; and among the first who insisted that the common cold is more likely to come from contagion than from exposure. As he put it in one of the notes he made [in] 1773 for a paper he intended to write: "Think they get cold by coming *out* of such hot rooms; they get them by being *in.*"

Though from 1773 to 1783 Franklin was so much absorbed in politics he had little time for general ideas, he had hardly signed the final treaty of peace with England when his mind was alert with bold conjectures again. Having seen the first ascent of human passengers in a free balloon, in Paris in November 1783, Franklin at once—and apparently alone among his contemporaries—foresaw the possibility of aerial warfare. This discovery, he wrote in December, might "give a new turn to human affairs. Convincing sovereigns of the folly of wars may perhaps be one effect of it; since it will be impossible for the most potent of them to guard his dominions. Five thousand balloons, capable of raising two men each, would not cost more than five ships of the line; and where is the prince who can afford so to cover his country with troops for its defence as that ten thousand men descending from the clouds might not in many places do an infinite deal of mischief before a force could be brought together to repel them?" As I speak armed forces in Europe are each hesitating to attack for fear of the very consequences Franklin foresaw at a glance.

Franklin's own age knew him as philosopher and sage, statesman and wit, and while delighting in his charm and grace thought of him as always a figure of weight and dignity. It remained for another century to take affectionate familiarities with him, and call him Ben Franklin—which only his immediate family ever did—as the century called other heroes Andy Jackson and Abe Lincoln. The homely anecdotes of Franklin's Autobiography gave him a homespun reputation which does him less then justice. There was little that was shirt-sleeved in his science or politics or diplomacy. His manners, as I have written elsewhere, "were as urbane and expert as his prose." His economical maxims give a wrong impression of his character, which was generous and at times lavish. "Avarice and happiness never saw each other," he wrote as Poor Richard. "How then should they become acquainted?" So far from making a great virtue of the cunning which has been often ascribed to him, Franklin as Poor Richard said that "Cunning proceeds from want of capacity"—meaning that truth was better. "Dr. Franklin," Henry Laurens wrote when the British ministers were warily looking for some one to treat with Franklin for peace in 1782, "knows very well how to manage a cunning man; but when the Doctor converses or treats with a man of candor there is no man more candid than himself."

Though Franklin was an excellent and successful business man, he retired from active business at forty-two and spent forty-two years more in the service of the public. He might have made a fortune if he had patented his stove or his lightning-rod. He refused to patent anything which he thought might be of benefit to mankind. As he did not hungrily gather wealth, so he did not cautiously guard his comfort or safety. It must never be forgotten that in his seventieth year Franklin might with decency have done what his more conservative son advised him to do: that is, retire from active affairs and let younger men settle the conflict between England and America. Instead Franklin, at the risk of peace and even of his neck, took his stand with the revolutionaries. Life with him began all over again at seventy. The older the bolder.

I shall take the liberty of reading the final words of my "Benjamin Franklin," in which I have done my best to reduce his qualities to their essence. "Franklin was not one of those men who owe their greatness merely to the opportunities of their times. In any age, in any place, Franklin would have been great. Mind and will, talent and art, strength and ease, wit and grace met in him as if nature had been lavish and happy when he was shaped. Nothing seems to have been left out except a passionate desire, as in most men of genius, to be all ruler, all soldier, all saint, all poet, all scholar, all some one gift or merit or success. Franklin's powers were from first to last in a flexible equilibrium. Even his genius could not specialize him. He moved through his world in a humorous mastery of it. Kind as he was, there was perhaps a little contempt in his lack of exigency. He could not put so high a value as single-minded men put on the things they give their lives for. Possessions were not worth that much, nor achievements. Comfortable as Franklin's possessions and numerous as his achievements were, they were less than he was. Whoever learns about his deeds remembers longest the man who did them. And sometimes, with his marvelous range, in spite of his personal tang, he seems to have been more than any single man: a harmonious human multitude."

D. H. LAWRENCE (1885–1930), English poet and
novelist, argues that the model for America which
Franklin created is materialistic, and restricted, and
muffles the creative spirit. America is tangled in "her
own barbed wire of shalt-nots." We should emancipate
ourselves from utilitarianism and, as Lawrence writes,
"let Hell loose." But is Franklin actually responsible
for the vulgar materialism thought to be American?
How convincing is Lawrence's case? Is his view of
Franklin a just one?*

D. H. Lawrence

The Ideal American?

The Perfectibility of Man! Ah heaven,
what a dreary theme! The perfectibility
of the Ford car! The perfectibility of
which man? I am many men. Which of
them are you going to perfect? I am not
a mechanical contrivance.

Education! Which of the various me's
do you propose to educate, and which
do you propose to suppress?

Anyhow I defy you. I defy you, oh society, to educate me or to suppress me,
according to your dummy standards.

The ideal man! And which is he, if you
please? Benjamin Franklin or Abraham
Lincoln? The ideal man! Roosevelt or
Porfirio Diaz?

There are other men in me, besides
this patient ass who sits here in a tweed
jacket. What am I doing, playing the
patient ass in a tweed jacket? Who am I
talking to? Who are you, at the other
end of this patience?

Who are you? How many selves have
you? And which of these selves do you
want to be?

Is Yale College going to educate the
self that is in the dark of you, or Harvard College?

The ideal self! Oh, but I have a strange
and fugitive self shut out and howling
like a wolf or a coyote under the ideal
windows. See his red eyes in the dark?
This is the self who is coming into his
own.

*From *Studies in Classic American Literature* by D. H. Lawrence. Copyright 1923, renewed 1951 by
Frieda Lawrence. All rights reserved. Reprinted by permission of The Viking Press, Inc. Pp. 19–31.

The perfectibility of man, dear God! When every man as long as he remains alive is in himself a multitude of conflicting men. Which of these do you choose to perfect, at the expense of every other?

Old Daddy Franklin will tell you. He'll rig him up for you, the pattern American. Oh, Franklin was the first downright American. He knew what he was about, the sharp little man. He set up the first dummy American.

At the beginning of his career this cunning little Benjamin drew up for himself a creed that should "satisfy the professors of every religion, but shock none."

Now wasn't that a real American thing to do?

"That there is One God, who made all things."

(But Benjamin made Him.)

"That He governs the world by His Providence."

(Benjamin knowing all about Providence).

"That He ought to be worshipped with adoration, prayer, and thanksgiving."

(Which cost nothing.)

"But —" But me no buts, Benjamin, saith the Lord.

"But that the most acceptable service of God is doing good to men."

(God having no choice in the matter.)

"That the soul is immortal."

(You'll see why, in the next clause.)

"And that God will certainly reward virtue and punish vice, either here or hereafter."

Now if Mr. Andrew Carnegie, or any other millionaire, had wished to invent a God to suit his ends, he could not have done better. Benjamin did it for him in the eighteenth century. God is the supreme servant of men who want to get on, to *produce*. Providence. The provider.

The heavenly store-keeper. The everlasting Wanamaker.

And this is all the God the grandsons of the Pilgrim Fathers had left. Aloft on a pillar of dollars.

"That the soul is immortal."

The trite way Benjamin says it!

But man has a soul, though you can't locate it either in his purse or his pocketbook or his heart or his stomach or his head. The *wholeness* of a man is his soul. Not merely that nice little comfortable bit which Benjamin marks out.

It's a queer thing, is a man's soul. It is the whole of him. Which means it is the unknown him, as well as the known. It seems to me just funny, professors and Benjamins fixing the functions of the soul. Why the soul of man is a vast forest, and all Benjamin intended was a neat back garden. And we've all got to fit in to his kitchen garden scheme of things. Hail Columbia!

The soul of man is a dark forest. The Hercynian Wood that scared the Romans so, and out of which came the whiteskinned hordes of the next civilization.

Who knows what will come out of the soul of man? The soul of man is a dark vast forest, with wild life in it. Think of Benjamin fencing it off!

Oh, but Benjamin fenced a little tract that he called the soul of man, and proceeded to get it into cultivation. Providence, forsooth! And they think that bit of barbed wire is going to keep us in pound forever? More fools them.

This is Benjamin's barbed wire fence. He made himself a list of virtues, which he trotted inside like a grey nag in a paddock.

1 **Temperance** Eat not to fulness; drink not to elevation.

2 **Silence** Speak not but what may benefit others or yourself; avoid trifling conversation.

3 **Order** Let all your things have their places; let each part of your business have its time.

4 **Resolution** Resolve to perform what you ought; perform without fail what you resolve.

5 **Frugality** Make no expense but to do good to others or yourself—i.e., waste nothing.

6 **Industry** Lose no time, be always employed in something useful; cut off all unnecessary action.

7 **Sincerity** Use no hurtful deceit; think innocently and justly, and, if you speak, speak accordingly.

8 **Justice** Wrong none by doing injuries, or omitting the benefits that are your duty.

9 **Moderation** Avoid extremes, forbear resenting injuries as much as you think they deserve.

10 **Cleanliness** Tolerate no uncleanliness in body, clothes, or habitation.

11 **Tranquility** Be not disturbed at trifles, or at accidents common or unavoidable.

12 **Chastity** Rarely use venery but for health and offspring, never to dulness, weakness, or the injury of your own or another's peace or reputation.

13 **Humility** Imitate Jesus and Socrates.

A Quaker friend told Franklin that he, Benjamin, was generally considered proud, so Benjamin put in the Humility touch as an afterthought. The amusing part is the sort of humility it displays. "Imitate Jesus and Socrates," and mind you don't outshine either of these two. One can just imagine Socrates and Alcibiades roaring in their cups over Philadelphian Benjamin, and Jesus looking at him a little puzzled, and murmuring: "Aren't you wise in your own conceit, Ben?"

"Henceforth be masterless," retorts Ben. "Be ye each one his own master unto himself, and don't let even the Lord put his spoke in." "Each man his own master" is but a puffing up of masterlessness.

Well, the first of Americans practised this enticing list with assiduity, setting a national example. He had the virtues in columns, and gave himself good and bad marks according as he thought his behaviour deserved. Pity these conduct charts are lost to us. He only remarks that Order was his stumbling block. He could not learn to be neat and tidy.

Isn't it nice to have nothing worse to confess?

He was a little model, was Benjamin. Doctor Franklin. Snuff-coloured little man! Immortal soul and all!

The immortal soul part was a sort of cheap insurance policy.

Benjamin had no concern, really, with the immortal soul. He was too busy with social man.

1. He swept and lighted the streets of young Philadelphia.

2. He invented electrical appliances.

3. He was the centre of a moralizing club in Philadelphia, and he wrote the moral humorisms of Poor Richard.

4. He was a member of all the important councils of Philadelphia, and then of the American colonies.

5. He won the cause of American Independence at the French Court, and was the economic father of the United States.

Now what more can you want of a man? And yet he is *infra dig*, even in Philadelphia.

I admire him. I admire his sturdy courage first of all, then his sagacity, then his glimpsing into the thunders of electricity, then his common-sense humour. All the qualities of a great man, and never more than a great citizen. Middle-sized, sturdy, snuff-coloured Doctor Franklin, one of the soundest citizens that ever trod or "used venery."

I do not like him.

And, by the way, I always thought books of Venery were about hunting deer.

There is a certain earnest naïveté about him. Like a child. And like a little old man. He has again become as a little child, always as wise as his grandfather, or wiser.

Perhaps, as I say, the most complete citizen that ever "used venery."

Printer, philosopher, scientist, author and patriot, impeccable husband and citizen, why isn't he an archetype?

Pioneer, Oh Pioneers! Benjamin was one of the greatest pioneers of the United States. Yet we just can't do with him.

What's wrong with him then? Or what's wrong with us?

I can remember, when I was a little boy, my father used to buy a scrubby yearly almanack with the sun and moon and stars on the cover. And it used to prophesy bloodshed and famine. But also crammed in corners it had little anecdotes and humorisms, with a moral tag. And I used to have my little priggish laugh at the woman who counted her chickens before they were hatched, and so forth, and I was convinced that honesty was the best policy, also a little priggishly. The author of these bits was Poor Richard, and Poor Richard was Benjamin Franklin, writing in Philadelphia well over a hundred years before.

And probably I haven't got over those Poor Richard tags yet. I rankle still with them. They are thorns in young flesh.

Because although I still believe that honesty is the best policy, I dislike policy altogether; though it is just as well not to count your chickens before they are hatched, it's still more hateful to count them with gloating when they *are* hatched. It has taken me many years and countless smarts to get out of that barbed wire moral enclosure that Poor Richard rigged up. Here am I now in tatters and scratched to ribbons, sitting in the middle of Benjamin's America looking at the barbed wire, and the fat sheep crawling under

the fence to get fat outside and the watchdogs yelling at the gate lest by chance anyone should get out by the proper exit. Oh America! Oh Benjamin! And I just utter a long loud curse against Benjamin and the American corral.

Moral America! Most moral Benjamin. Sound, satisfied Ben!

He had to go to the frontiers of his State to settle some disturbance among the Indians. On this occasion he writes:

We found that they had made a great bonfire in the middle of the square; they were all drunk, men and women quarrelling and fighting. Their dark-coloured bodies, half naked, seen only by the gloomy light of the bonfire, running after and beating one another with fire-brands, accompanied by their horrid yellings, formed a scene the most resembling our ideas of hell that could well be imagined. There was no appeasing the tumult, and we retired to our lodging. At midnight a number of them came thundering at our door, demanding more rum, of which we took no notice.

The next day, sensible they had misbehaved in giving us that disturbance, they sent three of their counsellors to make their apology. The orator acknowledged the fault, but laid it upon the rum, and then endeavoured to excuse the rum by saying: "The Great Spirit, who made all things, made everything for some use; and whatever he designed anything for, that use it should always be put to. Now, when he had made rum, he said: 'Let this be for the Indians to get drunk with.' And it must be so."

And, indeed, if it be the design of Providence to extirpate these savages in order to make room for the cultivators of the earth, it seems not improbable that rum may be the appointed means. It has already annihilated all the tribes who formerly inhabited all the seacoast . . .

This, from the good doctor, with such suave complacency is a little disenchanting. Almost too good to be true.

But there you are! The barbed wire fence. "Extirpate these savages in order to make room for the cultivators of the earth." Oh, Benjamin Franklin. He even "used venery" as a cultivator of seed.

Cultivate the earth, ye gods! The Indians did that, as much as they needed. And they left off there. Who built Chicago? Who cultivated the earth until it spawned Pittsburgh, Pa.?

The moral issue! Just look at it! Cultivation included. If it's a mere choice of Kultur or cultivation, I give it up.

Which brings us right back to our question, what's wrong with Benjamin, that we can't stand him? Or else, what's wrong with us, that we find fault with such a paragon?

Man is a moral animal. All right. I am a moral animal. And I'm going to remain such. I'm not going to be turned into a virtuous little automaton as Benjamin would have me. "This is good, that is bad. Turn the little handle and let the good tap flow," saith Benjamin and all America with him. "But first of all extirpate those savages who are always turning on the bad tap."

I am a moral animal. But I am not a moral machine. I don't work with a little set of handles or levers. The Temperance-silence-order-resolution-frugality-industry-sincerity-justice-moderation-cleanliness-tranquility-chastity-humility keyboard is not going to get me going. I'm really not just an automatic piano with a moral Benjamin getting tunes out of me.

Here's my creed, against Benjamin's. This is what I believe:

"That I am I."
"That my soul is a dark forest."
"That my known self will never be more than a little clearing in the forest."
"That gods, strange gods, come forth from the forest into the clearing of my known self, and then go back."
"That I must have the courage to let them come and go."
"That I will never let mankind put anything over me, but that I will try always to recognize and submit to the gods in me and the gods in other men and women."

There is my creed. He who runs may read. He who prefers to crawl, or to go by gasoline, can call it rot.

Then for a "list." It is rather fun to play at Benjamin.

1 **Temperance** Eat and carouse with Bacchus, or munch dry bread with Jesus, but don't sit down without one of the gods.

2 **Silence** Be still when you have nothing to say; when genuine passion moves you, say what you've got to say, and say it hot.

3 **Order** Know that you are responsible to the gods inside you and to the men in whom the gods are manifest. Recognize your superiors and your inferiors, according to the gods. This is the root of all order.

4 **Resolution** Resolve to abide by your own deepest promptings, and to sacrifice the smaller thing to the greater. Kill when you must, and be killed the same: the *must* coming from the gods inside you, or from the men in whom you recognize the Holy Ghost.

5 **Frugality** Demand nothing; accept what you see fit. Don't waste your pride or squander your emotion.

6 **Industry** Lose no time with ideals; serve the Holy Ghost; never serve mankind.

7 **Sincerity** To be sincere is to remember that I am I, and that the other man is not me.

8 **Justice** The only justice is to follow the sincere intuition of the soul, angry or gentle. Anger is just, and pity is just, but judgment is never just.

9 **Moderation** Beware of absolutes. There are many gods.

10 **Cleanliness** Don't be too clean. It impoverishes the blood.

11 **Tranquillity** The soul has many mo-

tions, many gods come and go. Try and find your deepest issue, in every confusion and abide by that. Obey the man in whom you recognize the Holy Ghost; command when your honour comes to command.

12 **Chastity** Never "use" venery at all. Follow your passional impulse, if it be answered in the other being; but never have any motive in mind, neither off-spring nor health nor even pleasure, nor even service. Only know that "venery" is of the great gods. An offering-up of yourself to the very great gods, the dark ones, and nothing else.

13 **Humility** See all men and women according to the Holy Ghost that is within them. Never yield before the barren.

There's my list. I have been trying dimly to realize it for a long time, and only America and old Benjamin have at last goaded me into trying to formulate it.

And now I, at least, know why I can't stand Benjamin. He tries to take away my wholeness and my dark forest, my freedom. For how can any man be free, without an illimitable background? And Benjamin tries to shove me into a barbed-wire paddock and make me grow potatoes or Chicagoes.

And how can I be free, without gods that come and go? But Benjamin won't let anything exist except my useful fellow-men, and I'm sick of them; as for his Godhead, his Providence, He is Head of nothing except a vast heavenly store that keeps every imaginable line of goods, from victrolas to cat-o-nine tails.

And how can any man be free without a soul of his own, that he believes in and won't sell at any price? But Benjamin doesn't let me have a soul of my own. He says I am nothing but a servant of mankind—galley-slave I call it—and if I don't get my wages here below—that is, if Mr. Pierpont Morgan or Mr. Nosey Hebrew or the grand United States Gov-

ernment, the great US, US or SOMEOFUS manages to scoop in my bit along with their lump—why, never mind, I shall get my wages HEREAFTER.

Oh Benjamin! Oh Binjum! You do NOT suck me in any longer.

And why oh why should the snuff coloured little trap have wanted to take us all in? Why did he do it?

Out of sheer human cussedness, in the first place. We do all like to get things inside a barbed-wire corral. Especially our fellow-men. We love to round them up inside the barbed-wire enclosure of FREEDOM, and make'em work. *"Work, you free jewel,* WORK!" shouts the liberator, cracking his whip. Benjamin, I will not work. I do not choose to be a free democrat. I am absolutely a servant of my own Holy Ghost.

Sheer cussedness! But there was as well the salt of a subtler purpose. Benjamin was just in his eyeholes—to use an English vulgarism meaning he was just delighted—when he was at Paris judiciously milking money out of the French monarchy for the overthrow of all monarchy. If you want to ride your horse to somewhere you must put a bit in his mouth. And Benjamin wanted to ride his horse so that it would upset the whole apple-cart of the old masters. He wanted the whole European apple-cart upset. So he had to put a strong bit in the mouth of his ass.

"Henceforth be masterless."

That is, he had to break-in the human ass completely, so that much more might be broken, in the long run. For the moment it was the British Government that had to have a hole knocked in it. The first real hole it ever had: the breach of the American rebellion.

Benjamin, in his sagacity, knew that the breaking of the old world was a long process. In the depths of his own under-consciousness he hated England, he hated Europe, he hated the whole corpus of the European being. He wanted to be American. But you can't change your nature and mode of consciousness like changing your shoes. It is a gradual shedding. Years must go by, and centuries must elapse before you have finished. Like a son escaping from the domination of his parents. The escape is not just one rupture. It is a long and half-secret process.

So with the American. He was a European when he first went over the Atlantic. He is in the main a recreant European still. From Benjamin Franklin to Woodrow Wilson may be a long stride, but it is a stride along the same road. There is no new road. The same old road, become dreary and futile. Theoretic and materialistic.

Why then did Benjamin set up this dummy of a perfect citizen as a pattern to America? Of course he did it in perfect good faith, as far as he knew. He thought it simply was the true ideal. But what we *think* we do is not very important. We never really know what we are doing. Either we are materialistic instruments, like Benjamin or we move in the gesture of creation, from our deepest self, usually unconscious. We are only the actors, we are never wholly the authors of our own deeds or works. IT is the author, the unknown inside us or outside us. The best we can do is to try to hold ourselves in unison with the deeps which are inside us. And the worst we can do is to try to have things our own way, when we run counter to IT, and in the long run get our knuckles rapped for our presumption.

So Benjamin contriving money out of the Court of France. He was contriving the first steps of the overthrow of all Europe, France included. You can never have a new thing without breaking an old. Europe happens to be the old thing. America, unless the people in America assert themselves too much in opposition to the inner gods, should be the new thing. The new thing is the death of the old. But you can't cut the throat of an epoch. You've got to steal the life from it through several centuries.

And Benjamin worked for this both directly and indirectly. Directly, at the Court of France, making a small but very dangerous hole in the side of England, through which hole Europe has by now almost bled to death. And indirectly in Philadelphia, setting up this unlovely, snuff coloured little ideal, or automaton, of a pattern American. The pattern American, this dry, moral, utilitarian little democrat, has done more to ruin the old Europe than any Russian nihilist. He has done it by slow attrition, like a son who has stayed at the home and obeyed his parents, all the while silently hating their authority, and silently, in his soul, destroying not only their authority but their whole existence. For the American spiritually stayed at home in Europe. The spiritual home of America was and still is Europe. This is the galling bondage, in spite of several billions of heaped-up gold. Your heaps of gold are only so many muck-heaps, America, and will remain so till you become a reality to yourselves.

All this Americanizing and mechanizing has been for the purpose of overthrowing the past. And now look at America, tangled in her own barbed wire, and mastered by her own machines. Absolutely got down by her own barbed wire of shall-nots, and shut up fast in her own "productive" machines like millions of squirrels running in millions of cages. It is just a farce.

Now is your chance, Europe. Now let Hell loose and get your own back, and paddle your own canoe on a new sea, while clever America lies on her muck-heaps of gold, strangled in her own barbed-wire of shalt-not ideals and shalt-not moralisms. While she goes out to work like millions of squirrels in millions of cages. Production!

Let Hell loose, and get your own back, Europe!

VERNON LOUIS PARRINGTON (1871–1929),
longtime professor of English at the University of
Washington and author of the prizewinning *Main
Currents in American Thought,* identifies Franklin with
the triumph of new social ideals. He emphasizes the
modernity of Franklin's economic and political beliefs.
A self-made man, Franklin was never blinded by the
pettiness of narrow middle-class ideas of his own day.
His career as a diplomat, according to Parrington, gave
him a full view of corrupt British politics and
convinced him that American independence was
inevitable. How does Parrington justify his favorable
portrait of Franklin? What achievements does he regard
as among Franklin's greatest?*

Vernon Louis Parrington

Franklin: An Early Social Scientist

There was a singularly dramatic fitness in the life and career of Benjamin Franklin. America has never been more worthily represented at old-world capitals than by this unpretentious commoner, drawn from the stock of the plain people. A plebeian in an aristocratic age, he was nevertheless, by common consent, first among colonial Americans in qualities of mind and heart. A wit and philosopher, rich in learning, charming in manners, ripe in the wisdom of this world, resourceful in dealing with men and events, he was one of the most delightful as he was one of the greatest men produced by the English race in the eighteenth century.

"Figure to yourself," he wrote in his seventy-second year, "an old man, with gray hair appearing under a marten fur cap, among the powdered heads of Paris. It is this odd figure that salutes you, with handfuls of blessings." An odd figure indeed in such a setting, but a figure that captured the imagination of Paris, as it has since captured the imagination of America; so novel as to seem romantic —a charming rustic philosopher who might have stepped out of the pages of Rousseau. And so the French aristocracy patronized *le bon homme,* and laughed with him at the affectations of this preposterous world, and made much of him for the zest that it discovered

*From *Main Currents in American Thought, The Colonial Mind,* Volume I by Vernon Louis Parrington, copyright, 1927, by Harcourt, Brace & World, Inc.; renewed, 1955, by Vernon Louis Parrington Jr., Louise P. Tucker, Elizabeth P. Thomas and reprinted by permission of the publishers. Pp. 164–178. Footnotes omitted.

in a novel sensation. It was the same odd figure that had stood at the bar of the House of Commons and matched his intelligence against that of celebrated English lawyers; the same figure that had been called in council by the great Pitt—who thought himself too great to learn anything even from Franklin; that had been lashed by the scurrilous tongue of Wedderburn; that had seen a thousand bribes dangled before him by Lord Howe and other gentlemen—a figure that seems strangely out of place in that old-fashioned Tory world, with its narrow sympathies and narrower intelligence. And yet considered in the light of social revolutions, what other figure in eighteenth-century Europe or America is so dramatically significant? The figure of the self-made democrat, with some three millions of his fellows at his back, and countless other millions to come, who was entering on a world-wide struggle for political mastery, the end of which no one can yet foresee? His presence in the councils of gentlemen was a tacit denial of their hitherto unquestioned right of supremacy. It was a rare personal triumph; but it was far more significant than that, it was the triumph of a rising class and a new social ideal.

Although Franklin's origins, whether Boston or Philadelphia, were narrowly provincial, his mind from early youth to extreme old age was curiously open and free, and to such a mind the intellectual wealth of the world lies open and free. From that wealth he helped himself generously, to such good effect that he early became an intellectual cosmopolitan, at ease with the best intellects and at home among the diverse speculative interests of the eighteenth century: the sane and witty embodiment of its rationalism, its emancipation from authority, its growing concern for social justice,

its hopeful pursuit of new political and economic philosophies, its tempered optimism that trusted intelligence to set the world right. No other man in America and few in Europe had so completely freed themselves from the prejudice of custom. The Calvinism in which he was bred left not the slightest trace upon him; and the middle-class world from which he emerged did not narrow his mind to its petty horizons. He was a free man who went his own way with imperturbable good will and unbiased intelligence; our first social philosopher, the first ambassador of American democracy to the courts of Europe.

Fortune was kind to Franklin in many ways: kind in that it did not visit upon him the fate that befell his elder brother Ebenezer, of whom Sewall noted, "Ebenezer Franklin of the South Church, a male-Infant of 16 months old, was drowned in a Tub of Suds, Febr. 5, 1702/3"; kind also in that it set him in a land where opportunity waited upon enterprise, and where thousands of kindred spirits were erecting a society that honored such qualities as he possessed. In England he must have remained middle-class, shut in by a wall of prejudice; but in colonial America he found a congenial environment. Like Samuel Sewall, he swam easily in the main current of colonial life, won increasing honors, until—as he naïvely remarked—he came more than once to stand before kings. How fortunate he was is revealed by contrast with the career of his great English counterpart and fellow spirit, Daniel Defoe, whose *Essay on Projects*—a classic document of the rising middle class—might well have been Franklin's first textbook.

The earliest literary representative of the English middle class, Defoe preached the same gospel of social betterment. With his head full of projects for the advancement of trade and the material well-being of his fellows, he preached the new gospel of practical efficiency to a generation of wits, going so far as to assert that the ideal statesman should be sought, not among gentlemen but among merchants, whose training in business affairs had made them shrewd judges of men and capable in dealing with practical matters. But the London of Queen Anne was not a place in which to rise by preaching efficiency. Defoe's day had not yet come in England, and in spite of great abilities and arduous labors he remained a Grub Street hack, the servant and not the counselor of aristocratic politicians. Instead of coming to stand before kings —like the more fortunate Franklin—he stood often before constables; instead of cracking his joke and his bottle at Will's Coffee House, he was forced to study the ways of the unprosperous at Bridewell. But if he failed in his ambition to get on, he found a certain solace in the vicarious realization of his ideal. Robinson Crusoe, the practically efficient man making himself master of his environment, was the dream of Daniel Defoe; Franklin was the visible, new-world embodiment of that dream.

It was Franklin's supreme capacity for doing well the things which his fellow Americans held in esteem, that enabled him to rise out of obscurity to a position of leadership. Before he should be intrusted with the confidence of his fellow citizens, he must prove himself worthy of such confidence, and even in colonial America the task was far from easy. In the wealthier communities society was exclusive and select—nowhere more so than in Philadelphia—and it could not be expected to view with approval the advancement of a printer-tradesman, especially if he were a member of the

plebeian anti-Proprietary party. It was an evidence of Franklin's discretion that he removed from Boston, where neither his father's chandlery shop, nor his brother's baiting of the ruling gentry, would serve his purpose. In Philadelphia, free from family entanglements, he bent himself to the task of securing a competence, understanding how easily the wheel turns on a well-greased axle; and by the time he had come to his early forties he had kept his shop so well that henceforth it would keep him. He was ready to do his real work in the world; and in the choice of that work he revealed the curious *flair* for the timely that was so characteristic. His extraordinary successes in the field of civic betterments gained him the good will of the commonalty, and his experiments in natural philosophy won the approbation of the gentry. Interest in scientific inquiry, particularly in physics, had spread widely in England since the founding of the Royal Society, and to be an authority on magnetism was as evident a mark of breeding in Georgian England as discriminating judgment in the matter of manuscripts and mistresses had been a sign of culture among Florentine cinquecentists. In establishing a reputation as a natural philosopher, therefore, Franklin not only was acquiring dignity at home, but he was providing himself with a sure passport to European favor. And it was the seal of European approval that finally won for Franklin the grudging recognition of the first families of Philadelphia. A few held out against him and to the day of his death regarded him with disapproval; but in the end his personal charm prevailed with all but a handful of elderly Tory ladies. So delightful a wit and so useful a citizen could not be dismissed as a pushing tradesman.

Franklin first entered politics as a

member of the popular party, then engaged in a bitter struggle with the Proprietors over tax matters, defense of the frontier, and other questions of acute popular concern. There was the usual colonial alignment between the back-country yeomanry and the town gentry; between the agrarian and mercantile interests; and the dispute had reached a point where the yeomanry determined to appeal to the King to convert the commonwealth into a Crown Colony. As one of the leaders of the popular party, Franklin was singled out for attack. A bitter election went against him, and he lost his seat in the Assembly, only to be chosen Colonial Agent to England, there to begin his long diplomatic career. Probably no other attack which Franklin suffered was so coarse or vindictive as this assault by the Proprietary party, led by the first gentlemen of Philadelphia, John Dickinson among them. Unpleasant as the experience was, it proved of service to Franklin, for it taught him how quickly the hornets would be about the ears of anyone who disturbed the nest of official perquisites; and this was worth knowing to a colonial diplomat on his first mission to a court and parliament where yellow jackets were uncommonly abundant.[1]

---

[1] "You know," wrote Franklin to his wife on the eve of his departure, "that I have many enemies . . . and very bitter ones; and you must expect their enmity will extend in some degree to you." He was forced to slip away and get secretly on board the vessel. His activities were reproved thus by a certain Tory lady:

  Oh! had he been wise to pursue
    The track for his talents designed,
  What a tribute of praise had been due
    To the teacher and friend of mankind.

  But to covet political fame
    Was in him a degrading ambition,
  The spark that from Lucifer came,
    And kindled the blaze of sedition.
              (In *Works*, Vol. VII, p. 267.)

He was nearly threescore when he set out on his diplomatic mission, which beginning modestly as temporary agent of the anti-Proprietary party of Pennsylvania, was to broaden immensely as the American difficulties increased, until he became in the eyes of all the world the spokesman of the colonial cause; first at London to King, Parliament, and people, and later at Paris to all Europe. It was a mission of discussion and argument, curiously illuminating to a colonial bred in a simple, decentralized world. Before he went abroad Franklin had been a democrat by temperament and environment; when he returned he was a democrat by conviction, confirmed in his preference for government immediately responsible to the majority will. Centralized Tory governments had taught him the excellence of town-meeting ways. At London he discovered widespread political corruption. It was a world flyblown with the vices of irresponsible power. The letters of Franklin are full of the scandal of bribe-taking and pension-mongering, of gross parliamentary jobbery. The elections of 1768 were a debauch, the brisk bidding of Indian nabobs sending the market price of parliamentary seats up to four thousand pounds. "It is thought," he wrote on March 13, "that near two millions will be spent on this election; but those, who understand figures and act by computation, say the crown has *two millions in places and pensions* to dispose of, and it is well worth while to engage in such a seven years lottery, though all that have tickets should not get prizes." To expect such a government to be swayed by appeals to justice or abstract rights was plain folly, Franklin very quickly learned. The colonial goose was there to be plucked, and gentlemen who gained their livelihood by skillful plucking would not easily be denied. "To get a larger field on which to fatten a herd of worthless parasites, is all that is regarded," wrote the celebrated London physician, Dr. Fothergill, to Franklin. Even war with the colonies might not seem undesirable to some, for "an auditor of the exchequer has sixpence in the pound, or a fortieth part, of all the public money expended by the nation, so that, when a war costs forty millions, one million is paid to him."

It was a bitter experience for one who had grown up in respect for England and veneration for English traditions. Franklin was not a man of divided loyalties, and his love of the old home was deep and sincere. He had many warm friends there, and the idea of American separation from the empire was profoundly repugnant to him. It was not till he was convinced beyond hope that America could expect from the English government nothing but ignoble dependence that he accepted the idea of independence. Again and again he complained bitterly of "the extreme corruption prevalent among all orders of men in this rotten old state." "I wish all the friends of liberty and of man would quit that sink of corruption, and leave it to its fate." "I do not expect that your new Parliament will be either wiser or honester than the last. All projects to procure an honest one, by place bills, etc., appear to me vain and impracticable. The true cure, I imagine, is to be found in rendering all places unprofitable, and the King too poor to give bribes and pensions. Till this is done, which can only be by a revolution (and I think you have not virtue enough left to procure one), your nation will always be plundered, and obliged to pay by taxes the plunderers for plundering and ruining. Liberty and virtue therefore join in the call, COME OUT OF HER, MY PEOPLE!" "The people of England . . . are just and generous," wrote his friend David Hartley, member of Parliament, "and, if it were put to the sense of the people of England, you would not be left in any doubt whether it was *want of will,* or *want of power,* to do you justice. You know the blot of our constitution, by which, to our disgrace, and to your misfortune, a corrupt ministry, sheltered by Parliamentary influence, are out of our immediate control. A day of account may come, when the justice of the nation may prevail; and if it comes not too late, it may prove a day of reconciliation and cordial reunion between us and America." He is blind indeed who cannot see in such experience the explanation of Franklin's later effort in Pennsylvania and in the constitutional convention to keep government in America responsive to the will of the people.

During the long years of his ambassadorship, so rich in intellectual opportunity, Franklin was intimately concerned with economics and politics, and he found in them subjects congenial to his talents. By temperament he was what we should call today a sociologist. He cared little for abstract reasoning, but much for social betterment; and this led him to examine critically current economic theory in the light of present fact. All his life economics was a major interest with him, and his several contributions entitle him to be regarded as our first important economist, the only one indeed before the nineteenth century. His chief guides in this little explored field seem to have been Sir William Petty, the statistician of the Restoration period, in his younger days, and the French Physiocrats in later years. He was the first American to abandon the traditional mercantile school—a generation before other American thinkers had repudiated it; and he was the first to ally himself with the rising school of *laissez faire.*

In the year 1729, when he was just turned twenty-three, Franklin entered the field of economics with a pamphlet entitled *A Modest Inquiry into the Nature and Necessity of a Paper Currency.* It is a curiously suggestive work, not only for the light which it sheds on his economic views, but on his social and political sympathies. It marks his early alignment with the agrarian party, to which he adhered to the end of his life. From the days when Samuel Sewall first confronted the question of land-banks in the Massachusetts legislature till the British government forbade all issues of bills of credit, the currency question was bitterly debated in the several colonies. It was primarily a class issue, in which the town merchants and money lenders found themselves outvoted by the agrarian debtors and small men. Little light had come from those debates on the nature of money and its social functions; but much heat had been engendered over the supposed question of honest versus dishonest money. With this cheap fallacy Franklin was not concerned; but he was greatly concerned in this and in later papers expounding the quantitative theory of money, the nature of credit, and the important fact, overlooked by the hard-money men, that gold and silver are themselves commodities, fluctuating in value with supply and demand. This first pamphlet, Franklin afterward remarked, "was well received by the common people in general; but the rich men disliked it, for it increased and strengthened the clamor for more money; and, they happening to have no writers among them that were able to answer it, their opposition slack-

ened, and the point was carried by a majority in the House.

By much the most interesting idea in the pamphlet, however, is the elaboration of the labor theory of value. Commenting on this, McMaster says in his *Life of Franklin:*

Bad as were his notions of political economy, his pamphlet contained one great truth, — the truth that labor is the measure of value. Whether he discovered, or, as is not unlikely, borrowed it, he was the first openly to assert it; and his it remained till, forty-seven years later, Adam Smith adopted it and reaffirmed it in "The Wealth of Nations."

Unfortunately the biographer's knowledge of the history of economic thought was as faulty as, in his judgment, were Franklin's economic principles. In his *Treatise of Taxes,* written in 1662, Sir William Petty—whom Franklin in many ways greatly resembled—clearly elaborated the principle of labor-value; it was restated by Vauban in 1707, in his *Projet d'une disme Royale,* by Hume in 1752, and later by the Physiocrats; and when Adam Smith wrote it was pretty widely known. There can be little doubt where Franklin got it. The similarity between his work and that of Sir William Petty is too evident to escape comment. But that does not lessen the significance of the fact that a self-trained provincial of three and twenty should have read Petty's work, seized upon the salient idea and turned it to effective use, years before economic students generally were acquainted with it. All his life Franklin took up ideas like a sponge, and what he took he incorporated with the solid results of his own observations.

During his stay in England Franklin came in close contact with the body of Physiocratic writings, which seem to have greatly stimulated his interest in economic thought. The school was at the height of its influence between the years 1763 and 1772, and had pretty well undermined the position of the mercantilists. They were the founders of modern social science and their teachings contained in germ the liberal doctrine of economics in its entirety. In their emphasis upon free trade and *laissez-faire* competition, on the police theory of the state, on property, security, liberty, on the natural laws of association and self-interest, and especially in their emphasis on land as the sole source of wealth, they presented a system of economics that fitted American conditions as Franklin understood those conditions. In one important point —their acceptance of an absolute prince— Franklin broke with them wholly; but their preference for agriculture over manufacturing and commerce accorded with his deepest convictions. America was notably happy and contented in comparison with Europe, and America would remain happy and contented, he believed, so long as land was abundant and her farmers remained freeholders. The new middle-cass gospel of industrialism he profoundly distrusted. He shared Goldsmith's concern over the destruction of the English peasantry and the creation of a degraded proletariat. Manufacture and trade developed only where free land was inadequate or the peasants were dispossessed; industrialism sprang from the national poverty and was nourished by it. Writing in 1760 he said:

Unprejudiced men well know, that all the penal and prohibitory laws that were ever thought on will not be sufficient to prevent manufactures in a country, whose inhabitants surpass the number that can subsist by the husbandry of it. . . . Manufactures are founded in poverty. It is the number of poor without land in a country, and who must work for others at low wages or starve, that enables undertakers to carry on a manufacture, and afford it cheap enough to prevent the importation of the same kind from abroad, and to bear the expense of its own exportation. But no man, who can have a piece of land of his own, sufficient by his labor to subsist his family in plenty, is poor enough to be a manufacturer, and work for a master. Hence while there is land enough in America for our people, there can never be manufactures to any amount or value.

Nine years later, in his *Positions to be Examined, concerning National Wealth,* he stated the Physiocratic theory thus:

There seem to be but three ways for a nation to acquire wealth. The first is by *war,* as the Romans did, in plundering their conquered neighbors. This is *robbery.* The second by *commerce,* which is generally *cheating.* The third by *agriculture,* the only *honest way,* wherein man receives a real increase of the seed thrown into the ground, in a kind of continual miracle, wrought by the hand of God in his favor.

Franklin's prejudice against trade somewhat lessened in after years, as he considered the economic need of free exchange of commodities. In 1774, two years before the publication of *The Wealth of Nations,* he collaborated with George Whately in writing a pamphlet entitled *Principles of Trade,* that suggests Adam Smith. Franklin was acquainted with Smith, had visited him, and doubtless had discussed with him the theory of *laissez faire,* division of labor, use of machinery, and other principles of the new school, but no mention of him is made. The central doctrine is thus elaborated:

Perhaps, in general, it would be better if government meddled no farther with trade, than to protect it, and let it take its course.

Most of the statutes, or acts, edicts, *arrêts,* and placarts of parliaments, princes, and states, for regulating, directing, or restraining of trade, have, we think, been either political blunders, or jobs obtained by artful men for private advantage, under pretense of public good. When Colbert assembled some wise old merchants of France, and desired their advice and opinion, how he could best serve and promote commerce, their answer, after consultation, was, in three words only, *Laissez-nous faire:* "Let us alone." It is said by a very solid writer of the same nation, that he is well advanced in the science of politics, who knows the full force of that maxim, *Pas trop gouverner:* "Not to govern too much." Which, perhaps, would be of more use when applied to trade, than in any other public concern. It were therefore to be wished, that commerce was as free between all the nations of the world, as it is between the several counties of England; so would all, by mutual communication, obtain more enjoyments. Those counties do not ruin one another by trade; neither would the nations. No nation was ever ruined by trade, even seemingly the most disadvantageous.

As a colonial, long familiar with the injustice of Navigation Laws, Boards of Trade, and other restrictions in favor of British tradesmen, Franklin agreed with Adam Smith on the principle of free trade; but with later developments of the *laissez-faire* school—its fetish of the economic man and its iron law of wages—he would not have agreed. Plugson of Undershot was no hero of his, and the social system which Plugson was creating would have seemed to him as vicious as the old system with its "bad, wasteful, plundering governments, and their mad destructive wars." In his later speculations he was rather the social philosopher than the economist, puzzled at the irrationality of society that chooses to make a pigsty of the world, instead of the garden that it might be if men would but use the sense that God has given them. "The happiness of individuals is evidently the ultimate end of political society," he believed, and a starvation wage-system was the surest way of destroying that happiness. In one of the most delightful letters that he ever wrote, Franklin commented on the ways of men thus:

It is wonderful how preposterously the affairs of this world are managed. Naturally one would imagine, that the interests of a few individuals should give way to general interest; but individuals manage their affairs with so much more application, industry, and address, than the public do theirs, that general interest most commonly gives way to particular. We assemble parliaments and councils, to have the benefit of their collected wisdom; but we necessarily have, at the same time, the inconvenience of their collected passions, prejudices, and private interests. By the help of these, artful men overpower their wisdom and dupe its possessors; and if we may judge by the acts, *arrêts,* and edicts, all the world over, for regulating commerce, an assembly of great men is the greatest fool upon earth. . . .

What occasions then so much want and misery? It is the employment of men and women in works, that produce neither the necessaries nor conveniences of life, who, with those who do nothing, consume necessaries raised by the laborious. . . . Look around the world, and see the millions employed in doing nothing, or in something that amounts to nothing, when the necessaries and conveniences of life are in question. What is the bulk of commerce, for which we fight and destroy each other, but the toil of millions for superfluities, to the great hazard and loss of many lives? . . . It has been computed by some political arithmetician, that, if every man and woman would work for four hours each day on something useful, that labor would produce sufficient to procure all the necessaries and comforts of life, want and misery would be banished out of the world, and the rest of the twenty-four hours might be leisure and happiness.

But the immediate problem of Franklin as representative of the colonies at St. James's, was political—how to reconcile the antagonistic ambitions of the sundered bodies of Englishmen; and the solution which he set forth with admirable clearness, bears the impress of a mind intent upon the reality behind parchment pretense. While lawyers were befogging the issue with legal quibble, and politicians were proving the unconstitutionality of the forces stirring in eighteenth-century America, Franklin was more concerned with adjusting imperial policy to existing fact. On one side were the colonies, in which the practice of local self-government had taken deep root; whether the practice was sanctioned by their charters or the British constitution was beside the question. On the other side was the British parliament, serving as a legislative body for its proper constituency, the people of the British Isles. Over both colonies and parliament, providing an effective but ungalling tie to bind the parts together, was the King, to whom both paid willing allegiance. So long as England was content to maintain the *status quo*, the colonies, Franklin believed, would remain loyal to the empire; but if the ministry persisted in its program of extending parliamentary sovereignty over the colonies, the outcome must be one of two things, federation or separation.

To the principle of federation Franklin was an early and faithful friend. The conception of a federal union of the several colonies was slowly spreading in America, and no other colonial had done so much to further it; in his well-known Plan of Union he had sketched the outlines of a federal constitution; what was more natural, therefore, than for him to think in terms of a Federated British Empire, as a statesmanlike solution of the present perplexities. The plan involved two problems: first, an inquiry into the nature and constitution of an imperial parliament, and second, provision for an equitable representation of the several divisions of the empire. The present difficulties had arisen out of the ambition of the British parliament to assume sovereignty over the colonial legislatures, thereby reducing them to a dependent status; those difficulties would be settled only by constitutional recognition of local rights and local sovereignties. "The British state," he argued, "is only the Island of Great Britain," and if by reason of familiarity with local needs, "the British legislature" is "the only proper judge of what concerns the welfare of that state," why does the principle not hold for the several colonial legislatures?

Here appears the excellency of the invention of colony government, by separate, independent legislatures. By this means, the remotest parts of a great empire may be as well governed as the centre; misrule, oppressions of proconsuls, and discontents and rebellions thence arising, prevented. By this means, the power of a king may be extended without inconvenience over territories of any dimensions, how great soever. America was thus happily governed in all its different and remote settlements, by the crown and their own Assemblies, till the new politics took place, of governing it by one Parliament, which have not succeeded and never will.

In this dream of a British Empire Franklin was far in advance of his time. On both sides of the ocean selfish and unimaginative men stood ready to thwart all such proposals; little Englanders and little colonials in vast numbers were concerned with more immediate and personal interests than those of the English race. Nevertheless Franklin was convinced that the gods, if not the Tories, were on the side of the colonies. The enormous increase in material strength that the years were swiftly bringing to America was an augury of good hope; the legitimate demands of America would be granted when America had grown too strong to be denied, which must be shortly. In the meantime it was the duty of Englishmen, British and colonial alike, to endeavor "with unfeigned and unwearying zeal to preserve from breaking that fine and noble China vase, the British empire." It was the traditional policy of "protract and grow strong"— a wise and sane policy—and Franklin clung to it until he was convinced of its utter futility. One other choice remained —separation; and he made that choice sadly, understanding better than most what it involved.

The years which followed were filled to the brim for Franklin as well as for America. Ideals changed and principles clarified swiftly; but his social philosophy was founded on too wide and sobering an experience with men and governments, to sway with every gusty passion of the times. He had been a democrat from his youth up and in those critical first days of independence, when the forces of agrarianism were taking possession of state governments, he threw in his lot with them, and joined heartily in the stimulating work of providing a democratic constitution for Pennsylvania. During the later years of reaction following the peace, when so many Revolutionary leaders endeavored to stay the agrarian movement and undo its work, he saw no cause to lose faith in government immediately responsive to the majority will. He was a forerunner of Jefferson, like him firm in the conviction that government was good in the measure that it remained close to the people. He sat in the Constitutional Convention as one of the few democrats, and although he was unable to make headway against the aristocratic majority, he was quite unconvinced by their rhetoric. For years he had been an advocate of unrestricted manhood suffrage, annual parliaments, and a single-chamber legislature; and when he heard eloquent young lawyers argue that a single-chamber legislature, responsive to a democratic electorate, must lead to mob legislation, and that good government required a carefully calculated system of checks and alances, he remarked:

It appears to me . . . like putting one horse before a cart and the other behind it, and whipping them both. If the horses are of equal strength, the wheels of the cart, like the wheels of government, will stand still; and if the horses are strong enough the cart will be torn to pieces.

When in 1790 it was proposed to substitute a bicameral system for the single-chamber in Pennsylvania, Franklin came to the defense of the simpler, more democratic form, with a vivacity little staled by years:

Has not the famous political fable of the snake, with two heads and one body, some useful instruction contained in it? She was going to a brook to drink, and in her way was to pass through a hedge, a twig of which opposed her direct course; one head chose to go on the right side of the twig, the other on the left; so that time was spent in the contest, and before the decision was completed, the poor snake died with thirst.

Both his economic principles and his views on government have been condemned by Federalistic critics as tainted with populism. They both sprang from the same root of agrarian democracy. Whether Franklin or his critics more adequately represented the larger interests of eighteenth-century America is beside the present question; it is enough to note that all such criticism is leveled primarily at Franklin's democratic philosophy as a thing in itself undesirable, if not dangerous.

Franklin may often have been wrong, but he was never arrogant, never dogmatic. He was too wise and too generous for that. In the midst of prosperity he never forgot the unprosperous. All his life his sympathy went out to whoever suffered in person or fortune from the injustice of society: to the debtor who found himself pinched by the shrinking supply of currency; to the black slave who suffered the most elementary of wrongs; to impressed seamen; to the weak and wretched of earth. He was a part of that emerging humanitarian movement which, during the last half of the eighteenth century, was creating a new sense of social responsibility. True to his Physiocratic convictions, Franklin was social-minded. He was concerned not with property or class interests, but with the common welfare; and in his quick sympathy for all sorts and conditions of men, in his conviction that he must use his talents to make this world better and not exploit it, he reveals the breadth and generosity of his nature. Reason and work, in his pragmatic philosophy, are the faithful handmaids of progress, of which war, whether public or private, is the utter negation. After long years of thought he rendered a judgment which later experience has not reversed,—"there is no good war and no bad peace."

It is to little purpose that certain shortcomings of Franklin are dwelt upon. "There is a flower of religion, a flower of honor, a flower of chivalry, that you must not require of Franklin," said Sainte-Beuve; a judgment that is quite true and quite obvious. A man who is less concerned with the golden pavements of the City of God than that the cobblestones on Chestnut Street in Philadelphia should be well and evenly laid, who troubles less to save his soul from burning hereafter than to protect his neighbors' houses by organizing an efficient fire-company, who is less regardful of the light that never was on sea or land than of a new-model street lamp to light the steps of the belated wayfarer—such a man, obviously, does not reveal the full measure of human aspiration. Franklin ended as he began, the child of a century marked by sharp spiritual limitations. What was best in that century he made his own. In his modesty, his willingness to compromise, his openmindedness, his clear and luminous understanding, his charity—above all, in his desire to subdue the ugly facts of society to some more rational scheme of things—he proved himself a great and useful man, one of the greatest and most useful whom America has produced.

I. BERNARD COHEN (b. 1914), Harvard historian of science, in analyzing Franklin's scientific achievements, concludes that Franklin's fame as a scientist in the eighteenth century was independent of his career as a printer and antedated his political activities as a statesman. Franklin's experiments in electricity established basic principles, so his reputation in his own time was very great indeed. Why, then, has Franklin's true stature as a scientist been largely overlooked by modern commentators?*

I. Bernard Cohen

Franklin the Scientist

The treatment of Franklin's scientific work by Americans presents a paradox to the historian of science. There is a vast array of books and monographs dealing with almost every aspect of Franklin's career and thought—his economic views, his political ideas, his literary style, his vocabulary, his service as postmaster, his diplomacy, his travels, his activities as printer, and so on—but no full-length work devoted exclusively to Franklin's scientific research. Until a decade or so ago there had never been an American edition of his book on electricity. Some excellent articles have presented information on specific aspects of Franklin's research, e.g., his contributions to meteorology, his studies of the Gulf Stream, or the date of his kite experiment, but the few general articles about his science have tended to link together his practical inventions and his contributions to electrical theory. Much has been said of Franklin the gadgeteer, and his "common sense." Many authors have pointed out that even in pure science he was more interested in knowledge for the sake of a possible application than for an understanding of nature, that his mind "turned ever by preference to the utilitarian and away from the theoretical and speculative aspects of things." Some warrant for this latter point of view has been found in Franklin's own words. He once wrote, "What signifies philosophy [i.e., natural

* From I. Bernard Cohen, *Franklin and Newton* (Philadelphia: American Philosophical Society, 1956), pp. 27–39. Footnotes omitted.

philosophy, or science] that doth not apply to some use?" And he also declared, "Nor is it of much importance to us to know the manner in which nature executes her laws; it is enough if we know the laws themselves. It is of real use to know that china left in the air unsupported will fall and break; but *how* it comes to fall, and *why* it breaks, are matters of speculation. It is a pleasure indeed to know them, but we can preserve our china without it."

Such quotations raise once again the question of the difference between what men say and what men do. . . . Removing these quotations from their contexts, and reading them without a due regard for the sentiments of the age, may give them a character wholly out of keeping with the aims and scope of Franklin's scientific research as revealed by an analysis of his actual contributions to science. In other words, an adequate interpretation of Franklin's (or any man's) scientific research can be obtained only by considering it in its entirety, by viewing it in the light of the thought of his times. Be that as it may, the fact remains that the best discussions of Franklin's contributions to science have not been produced by Americans but by European writers, notably the British and Germans.

I believe that one of the reasons for the neglect of Franklin as a scientist by American scholars, for the distorted view of his scientific career in American history books, may be found in the values which American society has placed on scientific research. It is a fact that during the first century and a quarter of national existence, America was not the birthplace of those leading scientific ideas and theories that revolutionized man's thoughts about the external world. But during this period, America produced a vast number of practical inventions, including the reaper, the sewing machine, the telegraph and telephone, and many others which radically altered the conditions of daily living, means of transportation and communication, and the methods of manufacturing and agriculture. Americans might well be proud of their achievements in technology during the nineteenth century. But among the names of truly great men of nineteenth-century science—Pasteur, Claude Bernard, Helmholtz, Faraday, Clerk Maxwell, Kelvin, Fresnel, Darwin, Koch, Cauchy, Gauss, Weierstrass, and Poincaré—there is but one American. Only Willard Gibbs achieved a scientific stature equal to that of the European giants. The century did see the appearance of notable scientific research by Americans here and there—Beaumont, Silliman, Henry, Hall, Asa Gray, and Rowland—but a comparison with Britain, France, or Germany would not place nineteenth-century America in the status of a major nation for its contributions to pure science. The most important scientific innovation to cross the Atlantic eastward was the introduction of surgical anaesthesia, but this revolutionary development, despite its profound significance, is in the area of practical innovation. I shall not explore the possible causes of the low state of scientific research in nineteenth-century America, but the fact itself must be noted because it is related in at least two ways to the view held by Americans concerning Franklin as a scientist.

In the first place, American historians of the nineteenth century, and those of the twentieth century who were influenced by them, were keenly aware that technical progress was a characteristic aspect of the growth of America and they consciously or unconsciously sought out roots of American inventiveness in the colonial period. Naturally enough, they were pleased to find Franklin producing useful inventions and household gadgets—the "long arm" (grandfather of the gadget used by grocers to take small boxes down from shelves), a stool that opened up into a ladder, a rocking-chair that fanned the reader while he rocked, a letter press, the "armonica," bifocal glasses (badge of many a library scholar), the lightning rod, and an improved form of stove which posterity has named in honor of the inventor the "Franklin stove," but which he called the "Pennsylvanian fire-place." An undue emphasis on such practical achievements has caused historians to neglect Franklin's contribution to pure or "useless" science.

The state of nineteenth-century American science produced a second effect on estimates of Franklin as a scientist, because the major American scientists of the late nineteenth and early twentieth centuries learned their science from European sources—chiefly German, British, and French—either by studying abroad or reading European works. Even the outstanding contributions of Willard Gibbs, though made in America, were introduced to American scientists through the medium of European commentators; Gibbs, furthermore, studied abroad before he made his great discoveries. The American scientific research of the twentieth century is, therefore, almost entirely built on the monumental achievements of nineteenth-century European science. Looking backward to the roots of their own scientific tradition, American scientists have seen only their immediate European masters. They have never found a direct chain leading back to the colonial period in America. Benjamin Franklin has not appeared to be a founding father of the scientific tradition of

American scientists. In point of fact, most American scientists do not even appreciate Franklin's major stature in the development of physical thought and would be hard pressed to explain how Franklin could ever have been considered a "Newton," save in jest.

Franklin as a Scientist, according to American Physicists

The recognition and support of pure science in America has been attained only by slow degrees and even today the victory is far from complete. A great majority of Americans, for example, still find difficulty in understanding why public funds for scientific research should not be used exclusively for investigations that will have "obviously" practical implications for medicine, for military purposes, or our economic well-being. Some shift in public opinion on the value of "pure" scientific research probably began after the Civil War. In 1875, at any rate, Joseph Henry optimistically reported a "great change" that "has taken place in the public mind as to the appreciation of the importance of abstract science as an element in the advance of modern civilization." What he had in mind was the "general" acceptance in 1874 of the character of the Smithsonian Institution, of which he was the founding Secretary, as an agency doing scientific research, whereas at the time of James Smithson's bequest (1835) "to the United States of America, to found . . . an establishment for the increase and diffusion of knowledge among men," the distinction between "original research and educational instruction in science and literature was scarcely recognized."

Two years after the end of the Civil War, Henry had written that the creation of a National Academy of Sciences during the war years marked the first recognition by the American government "of the importance of abstract science as an essential element of mental and material progress." A new means of acquiring "distinction" had been established; the "acquisition of wealth and the possession of political power" and "renown for successful military achievement" were—he thought—to be supplemented by scientific achievement.

By the end of the century, however, Joseph Henry's aspirations for science had not been fully realized. At the fiftieth anniversary meeting of the American Physical Society, held in Cambridge, Massachusetts, in June, 1948, a reprint of Henry A. Rowland's "Presidential address delivered at the second meeting of the society, on October 28, 1899," was distributed. This memorable document, entitled "The Highest Aim of the Physicist," is largely devoted to a defense of the ideal of "pure science" and an expression of hope that the future may witness an end to the deplorable condition, in which "much of the intellect of the country is still wasted in the pursuit of so-called practical science . . . and but little thought and money . . . given to the grander portion of the subject which appeals to our intellect alone." Looking in the past for names of Americans whom "scientists throughout the world delight to honor," Rowland found only four, despite the fact that he had searched the record for a period of more than a hundred years:

Franklin, who almost revolutionized the science of electricity by a few simple but profound experiments. Count Rumford, whose experiments almost demonstrated the nature of heat. Henry, who might have done much for the progress of physics had he published more fully the results of his investigations.

Mayer, whose simple and ingenious experiments have been a source of pleasure and profit to many.

We may note that three of the four men on Rowland's list—Franklin, Rumford, Henry—were in the "almost . . ." or "might have done . . ." category, while the fourth (whose name is just about completely unknown today) had produced experiments which Rowland assumed were well enough known to his auditors to require no further description. While Rowland appreciated that Franklin's work was of some importance, he obviously did not consider it of major rank.

Rowland's remarks formed the text for another address delivered before the American Physical Society at Cambridge, at the meeting of April, 1946. It was entitled "Fifty Years of Physics —A Study in Contrasts," and the speaker expressed the following judgment concerning the place of Benjamin Franklin in Rowland's list:

The many-sided Franklin, a legendary figure, had won fame along various lines. Had he not been famous as a publisher and a statesman, he might never have been heard of as a scientist. Balzac described him as "the inventor of the lightning rod, the hoax, and the republic." It has been maintained that there is no clear evidence that he ever performed the kite experiment, and it is certain that the experiment was performed elsewhere before Franklin wrote of it as a possibility. In any event, Franklin's work in science did not lack for publicity.

This statement is cited because it is typical of the sentiment of many American scientists concerning Franklin's place in the growth of modern physics. All too many physicists know of Franklin as a scientist only that he once flew a kite during a thunderstorm (an experiment apt to be chiefly remarkable because "Franklin was not killed at once") and that Franklin invented the lightning rod. Some few know, furthermore, that the designations used in electricity— "plus" and "minus" or "positive" and "negative"—are owed to Franklin, but this fact is sometimes mentioned in a derogatory fashion, since we would be better off if Franklin had reversed the names. If the lightning rod is an invention rather than a discovery, as Joseph Henry said, then Franklin's legacy to pure physics would seem to comprise the kite experiment and an error in nomenclature that is at present a source of unfortunate confusion.

Since the physicist's knowledge about Franklin as a scientist is so often limited to the kite experiment, the denial that he ever made this experiment (like the statement that the experiment was not original with Franklin) strips him of his only apparent claim to the high place given him by Rowland. Franklin does not, in these terms, seem to have a sufficient stature to warrant his being mentioned in the same breath with Newton.

Franklin as a Scientist, according to the American Historian

One further consideration is certainly relevant in a discussion of the treatment of Franklin by historians. When historians look back on the personalities of past ages, they cannot help but envisage reasonable types. A "universal genius" is not such a "reasonable type"; when one is supposedly encountered, as in the case of Leonardo da Vinci, great stress is apt to be laid on his failures: his unfinished paintings, the treatises never completed for publication. No man is allowed by history (or, perhaps, by historians) to accomplish too much. Now Benjamin Franklin was a man whose ap-

peal lies in the fact that he seems so human and alive, even after the passage of two centuries. He has been described as the only one of the founding fathers whom we might have wanted to greet by shaking his hand. Such a man might well do the things that other Americans do, and might even do them very much better. We are not particularly astonished to discover his wit and literary style, his skill as printer and newspaper editor, his sagacity in politics and diplomacy, and his efficiency in public service. As a trained craftsman, he was obviously talented at doing things with his hands, and it is completely reasonable that he was a talented inventor. Did not Jefferson too produce a variety of ingenious gadgets and inventions, like the improved plow? It was characteristic of the "age of enlightenment" for men to be interested in science. Jefferson's hobby of paleontology is almost as well known to historians as Franklin's kite experiment. So far and no farther does the "reasonable type" extend. No one would ever think of coupling the names of Jefferson and Darwin. The average historian would never conceive—much less understand—a similar coupling of the names of Newton and Franklin.

As the figure of a Newton is far removed from that of a "founding father" of the American republic, so the full measure of Franklin's importance in the growth of physical thought removes him completely from the simple, plausible human beings that we tend to re-create in the past. It is far easier to reduce Franklin's supposed "hobby" to its "proper" place. Evidence to support this reduction is available; historians point to the relatively few years Franklin devoted to intensive scientific research. Mention of the short time Franklin spent as a scientist is repeated in the secondary literature *ad nauseam;* but who else in the history of science has ever had the importance of his scientific achievement judged by the measure of time it took to do the research? Euler wrote so many books and articles that it seems as if a lifetime were too short for him to be able to write them all, much less revise them: but I know of no historian or scientist who has depreciated a single contribution of Euler's because it took so little time. No one would think of demoting Newton's scientific work to a minor position in the theory of thought because he abandoned science to work in the Mint and because even while he held his professorship in Cambridge he devoted a major part of his intellectual resources to the study of Biblical history, theology, and alchemy.

Franklin as a Scientist, according to the Historian of Science

One final consideration—perhaps the most important of all—that must be given its due weight in a discussion of modern views of Franklin as a scientist is the extreme youth of the history of science as a scholarly academic discipline. Historians of literature, philosophy, theology, political theory, and economic doctrine do not generally have much scientific training and experience; only in extremely rare instances is there an historian who has, say, studied any branch of science on the graduate level. Thus, even if the historian develops some interest in the history of science as it relates to his own research and teaching, all too often he is limited—especially in the science of the last 250 years—to whatever may be revealed by secondary works. The great primary documents of modern science—in physical science

such works as Newton's *Principia Mathematica,* Laplace's *Mécanique Céleste,* Fourier's *Théorie Analytique de la Chaleur,* Clerk Maxwell's *Treatise on Electricity and Magnetism*—are written in a mathematical language that most historians cannot read. Students of intellectual and cultural and social history are often eager to use the results of research in the history of modern science, but they cannot usually do such research themselves. Considering the lack of adequate and accurate interpretive works produced by competent, professional historians of science, one cannot but applaud the historians for the brave efforts they have made.

Few scientists today have the time, energy, or inclination to read the original documents in the history of science. There was a time, now passed, when it was held that such a study might have immediate practical value for the research scientist. The most vocal exponent of this view was the great physical chemist, Wilhelm Ostwald, and his famous series of *Klassiker der exakten Naturwissenschaften* was produced as part of his program to improve research technique, and eventually to establish a new science of discovery, based on the study and analysis of great scientific works of the past. No one, to my knowledge, holds with Ostwald's argument today, although in the past decades a number of scientists have come to appreciate the unique value of the study of the history of science for understanding the role of the scientific enterprise in our society.

Yet scientists often attempt to study the scientific documents of the past, despite their lack of historical training. Scientific books of two hundred years ago or more are written in a language that is different from that used in scientific books today. In order fully to understand and to evaluate the scientific writings of the time of Franklin, a knowledge of present-day electrical theory may be necessary but it is hardly sufficient. What is required is an appreciation of what other scientists were trying to do at that time, what the general scientific background of the era was: how the work in question was—in other words—related to the state of science itself at that time. To ask the scientist to steep himself in the science of the past is nothing other than to ask him to forego his scientific career and to become an historian of science. Clearly, the scientist, just like the historian, is hindered in his attempt to understand and evaluate the work of a man like Franklin by the lack of informed secondary works which would make the task feasible.

In the light of the important place of scientific enterprise in the making of modern civilization, many otherwise well-informed persons find it difficult to believe that the history of science is actually so young a discipline that scholarly research in this field has barely been initiated. A few examples will quickly show how true this is. The greatest scientist of the modern period—Isaac Newton—cannot be studied easily, because there has been no modern edition of his collected works; that made by Horsley in the eighteenth century is woefully incomplete, and does not include even a significant part of Newton's writings, or of his correspondence. Furthermore, there exists no critically annotated edition of any of Newton's major works; the two greatest of these, the *Principia* and the *Opticks,* although in print, are difficult to use even for the specialist. The same remarks apply to Lavoisier, the editing of his correspondence being only in the beginning stage. Innumerable

other major figures lack biographies, critical editions, or published correspondence. There are, lastly, all too few studies on the growth of science in America.

Once we recognize that serious study of the history of science has barely been initiated, we begin to appreciate why Franklin the physicist has been largely a neglected figure. Until now, it has been chiefly the historians, rather than the scientists, who have been interested in Franklin's experiments and theories. These historians have had to work without the guides and scholarly monographs to be found in all fields of learning save the history of science. No wonder that they have not been able to do justice to this aspect of Franklin's career! The stress often laid on the practical rather than the theoretical aspect of his work, the confusion of Franklin's inventions with his efforts in pure science, have produced an emphasizing of the "Franklin stove" and the lightning rod at the expense of the place of Franklin's thought in the age of Newton. But some historians would even have us believe that Franklin "directed" his scientific work so that it would have a practical outcome, or was interested only in aspects of science that would prove practical—thereby betraying nothing less than a woeful ignorance of the nature of scientific enterprise.

It has been mentioned earlier that some more or less adequate account of certain aspects of Franklin's research in electricity may be found in modern European books on the history of science. No one, who reads the material on Franklin in the books of Rosenberger, Hoppe, Whittaker, or Wolf, would categorize Franklin as a "practical" man or inventor at the expense of his contribution to experimental knowledge in electricity and to "pure" theory. Nor would any such reader reduce Franklin's impressive additions to electrical science to a single experiment (the lightning kite) and a new terminology.

Franklin as a Scientist, according to the Eighteenth-century Scientists

The author of every book on electricity in the latter half of the eighteenth century either referred to Benjamin Franklin by name—and not alone for his lightning kite and rod—or employed the concepts which he introduced into electrical science.[1] His book on electricity was one of the most widely read and admired treatises of its kind in the eighteenth century. Five editions were published in English, one in Italian, one in German, and a French translation went through two editions before a new and better translation appeared. Here is a genuine index of his scientific reputation, because these ten editions in four languages all issued from the press before the American Revolution.

In 1753 Franklin was awarded the Sir Godfrey Copley Gold Medal of the Royal Society of London for having "deserved well of the philosophical [i.e., scientific] world . . . [for] the experiments he has made . . . [and] the conclusions which he imagines may be deduced from them." Franklin was told he was "the first person out of the nation [England] that has had that honour conferred." In April, 1756, he was elected a Fellow of the Royal Society and given the unusual privilege of having his name "inserted in the lists before his admission [i.e., the admission ceremony], and without any fee, or other

payment to the Society. And that such name be continued in the lists, so long as he shall continue to reside abroad." In 1772, Franklin was elected *associé étranger* of the Académie Royale des Sciences, Paris, a particularly significant honor since, by the governing statutes of that society, there could be but eight such foreign associates at any one time; for one hundred years no other American was so honored. Evidence is abundant of the esteem in which his work was held by contemporaneous scientists.

Celebrated as a leader in the world of science from one end of Europe to the other, Benjamin Franklin's principles "bid fair to be handed down to posterity," as Joseph Priestly wrote, "as expressive of the true principles of electricity; just as the Newtonian philosophy is of the true system of nature in general." The "American Newton" was, even then, better known as a scientist in Europe than in America. Such words as "Franklinism," "Franklinist," and the "Franklinian system," it was said, occurred on almost every page of some Continental books on electricity. Silvanus Thompson noted in 1898 that electrophysiologists and electrotherapists "still indulge in the jargon of 'franklinization.'"

The facts concerning the reception of Franklin's electrical ideas in Europe show clearly that his reputation as a scientist was independent of his own activities as printer and actually antedated his career as a statesman. Franklin never printed his own electrical writings during the period of his most intense creativity; their partial publication in the *Philosophical Transactions* and *The Gentleman's Magazine* was entirely the result of independent action by his British admirers, who also arranged for the publication in England of his book. So, too, the translation of that book into French,

---

[1] By this I mean that even those authors who believed in a two-fluid theory of electricity, based their ideas on a pair of Franklinian fluids.

at Buffon's suggestion, was undertaken wholly on merit and without any personal intervention on Franklin's part; in fact, Franklin was pleasantly surprised by the news that a French translation had been made and published. To say, therefore, that had Franklin "not been famous as a publisher and a statesman, he might never have been heard of as a scientist," is absolutely wrong. Just the opposite is more nearly the case; his international fame and public renown as a scientist was in no small measure responsible for his success in international statesmanship. When Benjamin Franklin arrived in England in 1757 and again in 1764, or in France in 1776, he was not merely a representative of some provincial group, but a well-known figure with a commanding international reputation as a scientist. When Lord Chatham referred to Franklin's political ideas in Parliamentary debate, he compared him to "our Boyle" and "our Newton." The invention of the lightning rod, providing a device for preventing the destruction that had plagued mankind since time immemorial, of course made his name known on all levels of society, and it brought him a measure of fame among vast multitudes who could never hope to grasp the significance of theoretical physics. The demonstration that the lightning discharge, nature's mysterious and terrifying thunderbolt, was nothing other than the common laboratory spark discharge on a larger scale was particularly pleasing to the rationalist spirit of the day. It showed that experiment could eliminate common superstitions and fears. In an age in which kings, lords, and commoners were interested in science to a degree never before encountered in human history, Franklin, as one of the leading scientists of the age, met with a reception abroad that none of his American diplomatic colleagues could hope to command.

Comparing Science Past and Present

As we contemplate Franklin's scientific research in the age of Newton, we must keep in mind that the time in which he worked at electricity—the late 1740's and the '50's—was very long ago. A span of two centuries in modern science is difficult to bridge, even with a sympathetic eagerness to reach back to that state of knowledge and thought. In one sense, the physical science of antiquity or of the Middle Ages may be easier to grasp than that of the seventeenth and eighteenth centuries. Many of the concepts and postulates of distant ages are so totally different from ours that we can approach them freshly in their own terms without the encumbrance of our own preconceptions. But the physical science of the seventeenth and eighteenth centuries is largely our own science in its nascent form, and we cannot read any discussion written in those periods without attempting a translation of the ideas into our own more precise conceptual language and without making a comparison with our own more advanced state of understanding. It is difficult for us to appreciate the mighty effort required then to establish simple fundamentals that are taken for granted as "obvious" today. Yet, to make the achievements of the seventeenth and eighteenth centuries esteemed, we have only to see how many first-rate men struggled with them before a satisfactory result was obtained, however simple it may all seem in retrospect.

The fundamental postulate of the history of science is that the scientists of the past were just as intelligent as we are and that, therefore, the problems that baffled them would have baffled us too, had we been living then. Newton or Archimedes would have been a genius in any age. Yet since knowledge in science is cumulative, every college senior majoring in physics knows more about physics than Newton, just as Newton knew more physics than Archimedes. Archimedes could not have written the *Principia* because he lived too early, and Newton would not have written it had he lived in the twelfth century. But the average college senior majoring in physics would have written neither the *Principia* nor the works of Archimedes, no matter when he might have lived. And only a scientist of the first rank would ever have devised the experiments that Franklin performed, would have drawn from them the theoretical conclusions Franklin drew, and would have built thereupon the conceptual scheme. . . .

BERNHARD KNOLLENBERG (b. 1892), historian of early America and former attorney-at-law and librarian, believes Franklin was a philosophical revolutionist. He sees Franklin as a leader who questioned established religion and the mother country's governmental and taxation practices. Moreover, Franklin was never a spokesman for the wealthy conservative class in the colonies, although he was himself a wealthy man. How persuasive is Knollenberg's portrait of Franklin as a dedicated revolutionary?*

Bernhard Knollenberg

Franklin as a Political Philosopher

I am so much interested in Franklin that I accepted your invitation to speak in this series of Franklin Memorial Lectures without first inquiring as to my topic. I was later pleasantly surprised to learn that it was to be "Franklin as a Philosophical Revolutionist." This is a side of his character which is especially interesting to me and which has never been fully developed, though there are many sidelights on it in Mr. Van Doren's fine book.

Until the latter work appeared, the most careful study of Franklin's life was William Cabell Bruce's "Benjamin Franklin Self Revealed." Yet even Bruce profoundly misread Franklin's character in declaring that "By nature and train-

ing Franklin was profoundly conservative at the core." This means, I take it, that Bruce considered Franklin a person who tended to accept and adhere to the existing order of things, whereas, Franklin was in fact the very opposite of this. For from the beginning to the end of his life, we find him approaching every canon of thought or conduct with the question, "Is this logical? Does it hold water? Shall I be bound by it?"—no matter how old and generally accepted the idea, tradition or rule might be. True, he was cautious; he was shrewd; he was temperate. This, however, shows, I think, not that he was conservative but that he was wise; that he challenged the *status quo* with the approach of the philosopher; that, in

*From Bernhard Knollenberg, "Benjamin Franklin: Philosophical Revolutionist," in The Franklin Institute, *Meet Dr. Franklin* (Philadelphia, 1943), pp. 127–132.

short, he was a *philosophical* revolutionist.

My grounds for this view are numerous and diverse. To begin with, one of the relatively few things we know about Franklin's youth is that he early challenged the established religious teachings of his day. His first serious difficulty, when a boy of only fifteen in Boston, arose out of his articles in his brother's newspaper and some challenging remarks in conversation about religious matters. True, his brother's harshness to the young printing apprentice may have been a factor, but, to judge from the "Autobiography," the decisive reason for Franklin's taking French leave from his apprenticeship was that things were getting a little hot for him among those resentful of his rebellious, revolutionary attitude toward the religious tenets of the community.

Again, when he gets to Pennsylvania, we find evidence not only of the industry, economy, shrewdness in business we read and hear so much about, but also of his challenge to the established system of government in Pennsylvania. The wealthy and powerful Penn family, the proprietors of the province, their governor and satellites, were in a position to be most helpful to the ambitious Franklin by throwing printing business his way. But they were insisting that their relation to the colony was the same as that of the King to the royal colonies; that it would be as logically and legally indefensible for the legislature in Pennsylvania to tax the lands owned by the proprietors as for the legislatures in the royal colonies to tax the lands owned by the Crown. Franklin, approaching this question with his challenging mind, said: Why should these proprietors be exempt from taxation? As the community is developed, as peasants and yeomen come here from abroad and improve their lands, they are going to increase the value of these proprietors' lands. Why should the proprietors receive that increase in value, while paying nothing in the meantime towards maintaining the community that is enriching them? The revolutionist, Henry George, you will recall, stressed that idea many years later.

I do not contend that Franklin was unique in holding this view. It is one of those ideas that might strike any intelligent mind at any time. But I think it was original in the sense that it was Franklin's own insight and reasoning that led him to take this, at that time, revolutionary stand.

Franklin's approach to science was another illustration of his revolutionist tendencies. The outstanding scientists have, of course, all had challenging minds have all, in a sense, been revolutionists in their respective fields. But many able and useful scientists are not revolutionists. They may be teachers or conductors of research along previously well defined lines. Most of them would not, if they had lived in Franklin's time and place, have risked playing with the sacrilegious idea that lightning—that threat of divine punishment for the wicked, more immediately visible than hell fire—was really but a manifestation of the "electric fluid" which the experimentally-minded were having so much fun collecting in Leyden jars. But Franklin, with the boldness, the openness of mind, the determination to try to find and act on the truth, irrespective of tradition, that marks the revolutionist, made his great discovery that lightning was but a large-scale electrical discharge.

Though I am later going to give further grounds for my thesis that Franklin was a thorough-going revolutionist, I shall stop for a moment to contrast Franklin with some others who were of a somewhat different calibre, and point out the essential difference between their revolutionism and Franklin's.

As you think back over the famous revolutionists who have cropped up in history, you will recall that most of them were highly pugnacious persons. This is, I think, one reason that so many of them have been, or started out to be, lawyers; the same instinct for the argumentative that made the lawyers' profession attractive led them to challenge certain of the established tenets held by those around them. Such men are likely to be revolutionists in but a single chosen field, while remaining otherwise conservative. Furthermore, even within the special field in which they became celebrated they are likely to revert to conservatism. Luther, perhaps the most noted of these in the field of religion, is an example of this familiar type. Highly pugnacious and, in most respects, a hidebound conservative, he eventually became extremely dogmatic and inflexible even in the field of religion. Incidentally, Luther, as you probably recall, started out to be a lawyer. Another of the same kind was Patrick Henry. Having had his day as a political revolutionist, he eventually became one of the conservative leaders of Virginia.

Another group of revolutionists are those who, having suffered injury at the hands of the existing political or economic order, strike out against it in the frenzy of their anguish or in the desire for revenge. Thomas Paine, and most of the Russian revolutionists seem to have been of this type. This fact may account for the iron-bound rule into which after Lenin's death, the Russian Revolution appears to have developed.

Franklin does not belong in either of these categories. He had no bitter scores to pay off, and, far from his revolutionism being but a passing phase, we find him a consistent challenger throughout life. The question: Is the existing way the sound way, never ceased to ring in his ears.

Take the part in which he made his most enduring contribution: his part in the American Revolution. Franklin was not like Washington, a tobacco planter, exploited and knowing that he was exploited by the British law requiring his tobacco to be sent exclusively to Britain, thereby restricting his market and reducing his profits. He was not a large owner of slaves, one of whose essential elements of food—salt—and most of whose clothing —the rough Osnaburg cloth—coming from the continent of Europe, must be imported through Great Britain so that the British merchant could take his toll. (I do not mean to imply by this comparison that economic motives alone swayed Washington, but his letters show how important a part they played in forming his views.) Franklin was a clear gainer from his connection with the British Empire.

He held a lucrative job in the British Colonial Post Office Department. His newspapers flourished in part as a result of his connections with the British Government. His son, William, was appointed by the King to the governorship of New Jersey. When Franklin looked at the British government from the standpoint of gain or loss to himself, he must have realized that he was a beneficiary, not a victim, of the connection. Yet when the question of British taxation began acutely to present itself, we find his revolutionary character, his inevitable challenge to the existing, but logically indefensible order, slowly but surely unfolding.

In his first published statement on the matter in 1766, at the time the repeal of the Stamp Act was under consideration, Franklin said in his famous hearing before the House of Commons:

I never heard any objection to the right of laying duties to regulate commerce; but a right to lay internal taxes was never supposed to be in Parliament, as we are not represented there.

Although he may conceivably have been concealing his feelings, I think it fair to assume that this was Franklin's honest approach to the question.

Later, after thinking the matter over more carefully, we find him writing on March 13, 1768, to his son William,

The more I have thought and read on the subject the more I find myself confirmed in the opinion that no middle doctrine can be well maintained, I mean not clearly with intelligible arguments. Something might be made of either of the extremes; that Parliament has a power to make *all laws* for us or that it has a power to make *no laws* for us; and I think the argument for the latter more numerous and weighty, than those for the former.

Two years later we find a further development. At that time, in writing to an old friend—Samuel Cooper—Franklin is no longer balancing things this way and that. He says flatly

I could wish that such Expressions as the Supreme Authority of Parliament . . . were no longer seen in our publick Pieces. They . . . tend to confirm a Claim of Subjects in one Part of the King's Dominions to be Sovereign over their Fellow Subjects in another Part of his Dominions, when in truth they have no such Right, and their Claim is founded only in Usurpation.

He concedes that the King has certain rights as the source of the colonial charters, but maintains that Parliament as a law-making body had no power whatsoever over the colonies.

From this it was an easy transition to the view, expressed in a letter to Thomas Cushing, Speaker of the House of Representatives in Massachusetts, July 1773, in which, for the first time, Franklin puts himself squarely on record in favor of a program smacking strongly of treason. He writes Cushing that the Colonies

should engage with each other that they will never grant Aids to the Crown in any General War, till those rights are recognized by the King and both Houses of Parliament; communicating at the same time to the Crown this their Resolution.

The next step was, of course, the final one of open rebellion, when in 1776, as might be expected, we find Franklin among the five members of Congress who drafted the Declaration of Independence. Unlike some of the other prominent signers, however, there was, in Franklin's case, no relapse into conservatism. Death alone put an end to his challenging mind and the readiness to follow wherever the challenge might lead him. In November 1789, when Pennsylvania was going through the throes of a great constitutional crisis, the question arose whether a second house should be added to the Pennsylvania Legislature, to represent, not the people as a whole, but the wealth of the State. The wealthy—and Franklin was at the time one of the wealthy men of the State—were thus in effect to have a veto power over the legislation passed by the "mobility." But Franklin strongly opposed the bill, and, replying to an article in the Federal Gazette of November 3, 1789, wrote in a memorandum headed "Queries and Remarks":

And why is property to be represented at all? The accumulation of property and its security to individuals in every society must be in effect the protection afforded it by the joint strength of the society in the execution of its laws. Private property, therefore, is a creature of society and is subject to the call of that society whenever its necessities shall require, even to its last farthing.

This is a doctrine not far from Karl Marx's "from each according to his abilities, to each according to his needs" of a half century later; a doctrine which Lenin and some other well-known revolutionists have put into action in our present century.

To come back then to the statement of Bruce, I think that he must have been making the common error of using the term "conservative" as the equivalent of cautious, temperate, philosophic, wise. Franklin was all of these, but, far from being "at the core," a conservative, he was a revolutionist of extraordinary consistency.

DAVID LEVIN (b. 1921), University of Virginia specialist in American studies, believes that Franklin's *Autobiography* can be very misleading to the reader who does not understand why or how it was written. It is not fictional, yet it is a work of art in which the author sees himself from an outside perspective. Franklin, according to Levin, created an image of himself that reflected Puritan ideals of frugality, simplicity, and hard work. He wanted others to profit from his experience. Was Franklin's image in the *Autobiography,* as Levin argues, more materialistic and more naïve than Franklin himself? How convincing is Levin's treatment of the *Autobiography?**

David Levin

Franklin: Experimenter in Life and Art

It would be difficult to find a book that seems more widely understood, as a model of plain exposition of character, than *The Autobiography of Benjamin Franklin.* Everyone knows that this is the life of a self-made, self-educated man and that *Poor Richard's Almanac* was a best-seller. Everyone knows that the penniless sixteen-year-old boy who first walked down the streets of Philadelphia with his pockets bulging with shirts and stockings, and with two great puffy rolls under his arms, worked so diligently at his calling that for him the promise of Scripture was fulfilled, and he one day stood before kings. (He "stood before five," he wrote later, with characteristic precision, and sat down to dine with one.)

We all know, too, that the Franklin stove and bifocals and the electrical experiments bear witness to Franklin's belief in life-long education, and that it was because of his ability to explain clearly and persuade painlessly—even delightfully—that his international reputation soared higher than his famous kite.

Too often, however, we forget a few simple truths about this great man and his greatest works. We forget the chief purposes for which he wrote his autobiography, and the social system that led him to conceive such aims. Remembering his plainness, his clarity, we overlook the subtlety of his expression, his humor, and his qualifying statements. Above all, we forget that he was a writer,

* From David Levin, "The Autobiography of Benjamin Franklin, The Puritan Experimenter in Life and Art," *The Yale Review,* Vol. LIII, No. 2 (Winter, 1964), pp. 258–275.

that he had a habit of creating characters. And so he takes us in. Some of us forget that Poor Richard is just as clearly Franklin's creation as is Mrs. Silence Dogood, the fictitious character through whom young Benjamin had published in his brother's newspaper in Boston; many of us forget that *The Way to Wealth,* Franklin's brilliantly successful collection of economic proverbs, is a humorous *tale* narrated by Poor Richard, who at first makes fun of himself and then reports the long speech made by another fictitious character named Father Abraham; and most of us overlook the crucial distinction, especially in the first half of Franklin's autobiography, between the *writer* of the book and the chief *character* he portrays.

Please understand that I do not mean to call Franklin's autobiography a work of fiction. I must insist, however, that we refuse to let its general fidelity to historical fact blind us to the author's function in creating the character who appears in the book. Franklin's first entry into Philadelphia may serve as an example. We are apt to consider the picture of that boy as a natural fact of history, as if no conceivable biographer could have omitted it. It merges in our experience with the myth that Horatio Alger exploited a century later, and with dozens of other pictures of successful men at the beginning of their careers: the country boy walking into the big city, the immigrant lad getting off the boat and stepping forth in search of his fortune. So grandly representative is this human experience that our current critical fashion would call it archetypal. But it was Franklin the writer who elected to describe this picture, and who made it memorable. He was not obliged to include it. He *chose* to make it represent an important moment in his life, and he chose to depict his young former

self in particular detail. His dirty clothes, his bulging pockets, and the huge rolls constitute nearly the only details respecting his personal appearance in the entire book. He might have omitted them, and he might have ignored the whole incident.

If we try to imagine what our view of Franklin might have been had he not written his autobiography, we will recognize that the author's conception of himself has considerably more literary significance than one can find in a single descriptive passage. Though the honest autobiographer refuses to invent fictitious incidents, he *actually creates himself as a character.* He selects incidents and qualities for emphasis, and discards or suppresses others. He portrays himself in relation to some other character (whom he also "creates" in this book), but refrains from portraying himself in relation to some others whom he once knew. He decides on the meaning of his life and the purpose of his book, and he selects traits, incidents, and characters accordingly. Obviously he cannot record everything that happened unless he spews forth every feeling, impulse, twitch that ever entered his mind or affected his senses. Indeed, the very conception of a happening requires some selection, some ordering of experience and a point of view from which to perceive that order. D. H. Lawrence did not understand Franklin's autobiography, but he saw that it recognized a kind of order, and a view of the self, which imposed a planned control on natural feelings. "The ideal self!" he cried scornfully in his critique of Franklin.

Oh, but I have a strange and fugitive self shut out and howling like a wolf or a coyote under the ideal windows. See his red eyes in the dark? This is the self who is coming into his own.

The perfectibility of man, dear God! When

every man as long as he remains alive is in himself a multitude of conflicting men. Which of these do you choose to perfect, at the expense of every other?

Old Daddy Franklin will tell you. He'll rig him up for you, the pattern American. Oh, Franklin was the first downright American.

As we shall see later on, this gross caricature of "the sharp little man" reflects some imperfections in Franklin's ability to communicate with ages beyond his own, and as we shall see even sooner, it reflects an inability or unwillingness in Lawrence and many others to read carefully. For the moment, however, let us content ourselves with two observations in support of Lawrence's limited perception. First, Franklin's autobiography represents that kind of art in which the author tries to understand himself, to evaluate himself, to see himself, in a sense, from outside; it is a *portrayal* of the self rather than simply an *expression* of current feeling or an outpouring of those multiple selves that Lawrence celebrates. Old Daddy Franklin did indeed know what he was about. But the second observation must limit the praise in the first. The very terms in which Franklin expresses his admirable self-awareness limit his communication in a way that obscures the identity of the author. The technique of humor, and the disarming candor about techniques of influence and persuasion—these occasionally make us wonder which of several selves Benjamin Franklin is.

Franklin's art is deceptive. At first there may seem to be none at all. The book, written at four different times from 1771 to 1790, the year Franklin died, is loosely constructed; it is almost conversational in manner. It begins, indeed, as a letter to Franklin's son. It is episodic, anecdotal. Clearly, however, its narra-tive order includes two major divisions: the first half of the book describes his education, as he strives for a secure position in the world and for a firm character; the second half concentrates on his career of *public* service; though the account breaks off well before the American Revolution.

That simple pattern itself illustrates the most important fact about Franklin's autobiography. He not only creates an attractive image of himself but uses himself as a prototype of his age and his country. There are three essential ways in which he establishes this story of the self-made man securely in the broadest experience of his time. If we examine them with some care, we may understand his purposes and his achievement more clearly.

The first context is that of Puritanism, represented here by Franklin's admiration for John Bunyan's *Pilgrim's Progress* and Cotton Mather's *Essays To Do Good*. Although Franklin says that he was converted to Deism by some anti-Deistic tracts in his Presbyterian father's library, we cannot overestimate the importance of his Puritan heritage, and his own account gives it due credit. (I refer, of course, not to the gross distortion suggested by the word "puritanical," the joy-killing and fanatical, but to that firm tradition that required every Christian to venture into this world as a pilgrim, doing right for the glory of God.) It is to this tradition that we owe Franklin's great proverb "Leisure is time for doing something useful," his emphasis on diligence in one's calling, the moral preoccupation that colors his view of ordinary experience. We see the Puritan influence in his insistence on frugality, simplicity, and utility as standards of value; and we see it just as clearly in his acceptance of public duty, his constant effort to improve the community, his willingness at last to serve the local and international community without pay. When we remember that the Protestant ethic combines the profit motive with religious duty, we should remember that in Franklin's day (as in John Winthrop's before him) it also obliged one to use one's fortune, and one's own person, in public service.

The Puritan tradition, indeed, gave Franklin a more purely literary kind of model. By the time he was growing up there existed in both old and New England a fairly large body of personal literature that emphasized objective self-examination and the need to keep an objective record of divine Providence as it affected an individual life. One recorded one's daily life in order to evaluate one's conduct and also to find evidence of God's will in the pattern of events. It was the Puritan custom, moreover, to improve every opportunity to find moral instruction and signs of universal meaning in particular experience. Franklin himself describes and exemplifies this custom in an anecdote (not in the *Autobiography,* but in a letter) of a visit that he made in 1724 to the old Puritan minister Cotton Mather. As Franklin was leaving, he wrote later, Mather

showed me a shorter way out of the house, through a narrow passage, which was crossed by a beam overhead. We were talking as I withdrew, he accompanying me behind, and I turning partly towards him when he said hastily, "STOOP, STOOP!" I did not understand him till I felt my head against the beam. He was a man that never missed any occasion of giving instruction, and upon this he said to me: "You are young, and have the world before you; STOOP as you go through it, and you will miss many hard thumps." This advice, thus beat into my head, has frequently been of use to me, and I often think of it when I see pride mortified and misfortunes brought upon people by carrying their heads too high.

One of the most successful devices that Franklin uses in his autobiography is this kind of symbolic anecdote, or parable; what brings Franklin's practice closer to Puritan preaching than to the parables in the Bible is his careful addition of a conclusion that drives home the point—the application or use—for those who might otherwise misunderstand it.

Before turning from Puritanism to a second quality of eighteenth-century experience, we should pause for another minute over the name of John Bunyan. For the first half of Franklin's autobiography, as Charles Sanford has said, represents a kind of pilgrim's progress. As his pious contemporaries Jonathan Edwards and John Woolman published accounts of their growth in Christian grace, so Franklin, acknowledging the aid of Providence, narrates the progress of a chosen, or at least fortunate, and often undeserving young man through a series of perils (including the valley of the shadow of death) to a relatively safe moral haven, if not to the Heavenly City. Others, we must remember, do not fare so well. A number of his early associates fall into one pit or another, and although Franklin tries to show what he did to save himself, so that others might profit by his example, he makes it perfectly clear that on several occasions he was so foolish that he too would have gone down had he not been preserved by Providence —or plain good luck.

It is this sense of the perils facing a young man in the free society of the new capitalism that brings me to the second of my three kinds of representativeness. Whether he was a Puritan or not, the young indentured servant, the young apprentice, the young artisan or farmer of Franklin's time had to walk a perilous way in the world. And if, like a great many Americans, he was leaving his childhood community as well as the restraints and comforts of his childhood religious faith, when he came forth to make his way in the world, he faced those dangers with very little help from outside himself. He had precious little help in the experience of others, for often his experience was new for the entire society. The mistakes he made did not entitle him to the protection of bankruptcy laws or of the less grand comforts of our welfare state. They sent him to a debtor's prison, or subjected him to the permanent authority of a creditor. Franklin described plain economic fact as well as moral truth when he said, "It is hard for an empty sack to stand upright."

Thus one of Franklin's major purposes in the *Autobiography* was to instruct the young, not only by good example but by warning. Especially in his account of his youth, he presents himself repeatedly as the relatively innocent or ignorant young man in conflict with those who would take advantage of him. Much of the sharp dealing that annoys D. H. Lawrence and others occurs in this kind of situation. Franklin's older brother, exploiting and sometimes beating the young apprentice, tries to circumvent a court ruling against his newspaper by freeing young Benjamin and making him nominal owner of the paper; Benjamin takes advantage of the opportunity by going off to Philadelphia to strike out on his own. Samuel Keimer uses Franklin to train other printers so that Franklin's services may then be dispensed with; but Franklin plans to set up his own shop, and when he does, he prospers as Keimer fails.

As in the fiction of Daniel Defoe, whom Franklin admired, and Samuel Richardson, whom he was among the first American printers to publish, Franklin's *Autobiography* indicates clearly that the relations between the sexes concealed some of the chief dangers to the young freeman's liberty. Luckily, he concedes, he escaped the worst consequences of occasional encounters with "low women"; but in a society that frankly recognized marriage as an economic contract he was almost entrapped by a clever pair of parents who seem to have counted on hoodwinking the young lad because he had to bargain for himself in a matter that required cooler heads. Franklin's account of the episode is priceless:

Mrs. Godfrey [his landlady] projected a match for me with a relation's daughter, took opportunities of bringing us often together, till a serious courtship on my part ensued, the girl being in herself very deserving. The old folks encouraged me by continued invitations to supper and by leaving us together, till at length it was time to explain. Mrs. Godfrey managed our little treaty. I let her know that I expected as much money with their daughter as would pay off my remaining debt for the printing house, which I believe was not then above a hundred pounds. She brought me word they had no such sum to spare. I said they might mortgage their house in the Loan Office. The answer to this after some days was that they did not approve the match; that on enquiry of Bradford [another printer] they had been informed the printing business was not a profitable one, the types would soon be worn out and more wanted; that Samuel Keimer and D. Harry had failed one after the other, and I should probably soon follow them; and therefore I was forbidden the house, and the daughter shut up. Whether this was a real change of sentiment or only artifice, on a supposition of our being too far engaged in affection to retract and therefore that we should steal a marriage, which would leave them at liberty to give or withhold what they pleased, I know not. But I suspected the motive, resented it, and went no more. Mrs. Godfrey brought me afterwards

some more favourable accounts of their disposition and would have drawn me on again,
but I declared absolutely my resolution to
have nothing more to do with that family.

This anecdote is not among the most
popular with modern readers. It should
be noticed, however, that people who
owned their house outright did not
ordinarily leave their daughter alone
with a young man until they had some
assurance of his economic eligibility
for marriage, and that these parents were
not worried about Franklin's ability to
provide for their daughter until he
demanded the usual dowry. We should
notice, too, that the young Franklin who
is described in this anecdote seems at
last to have obeyed his own feelings of
resentment rather than the economic
interest that might have been served
by allowing the girl's parents to re-open
negotiations.

But although he always prospers, the
innocent young man is not infallibly
wise. Although he is never so roguish
as Moll Flanders, his confession appears
to be remarkably candid. He concedes
that he was greatly deceived by the
Governor of Pennsylvania, who sent him
as a very young man to England, along
with supposed letters of recommendation
and letters of credit that never arrived.
(That, by the way, was probably the
greatest peril of Franklin's young life,
and he confesses that he walked into it
despite his father's clear warning). He
admits freely to motives and perceptions
that we, along with most of his contemporaries, prefer to conceal. He thanks
heaven for vanity, "along with the other
comforts of life," and admits that it is
useful to cultivate not only the reality
but the *appearance* of industry and
humility. It was effective, he says, to
carry his own paper stock through the
streets in a wheelbarrow, so that people

could see how hard he was willing to
work. A book, he confesses, "sometimes
debauch'd me from my work, but that
was seldom, snug, and gave no scandal."

This apparent honesty leads us to the
heart of the book. My third kind of
representativeness, the most important
of all, can be summed up in a single
statement that appears near the end of
the *Autobiography*. "This," Franklin
wrote, "is an age of experiments." It *was*
an age of experiments, an age of empirical
enlightenment, when every freeman
might, if wary and lucky, learn by experience and test for himself. Franklin's
greatest achievement in this book is that
of characterizing himself repeatedly as
a man of inquiry. He creates for us a
convincing image of the inquiring man,
self-educated, testing for himself, in
morality, in business, in religion, in
science. On almost every page we see
some evidence of his willingness to learn.
He contrives to reveal the vast range of
his interests—from the pure science of
electricity, to the effect of lading on the
speed of merchant ships, to street-lighting
and street-cleaning, to the value of learning modern romance languages before
trying to learn Latin—all these he contrives to reveal in anecdotes of questioning and discovery. And in anecdote after
anecdote, the plain questioning of Benjamin Franklin in action applies an
experimental test to theories and assumptions. As a young journeyman printer in
England, he demonstrates to his fellow
workmen that the customary beer is not
necessary to the maintenance of strength;
he drinks water, and carries more type
than they can carry. Young Franklin and
a friend agree that the one who dies first
will prove the possibility of communicating from beyond the grave by getting in
touch with the other who remains alive;
but, Old Franklin the narrator reports,

"he never fulfilled his promise." As a military commander at the start of the Seven Years' War with France, Franklin hears the zealous Presbyterian chaplain's complaint that the men do not attend religious services; he solves the problem by persuading the chaplain himself to serve out the men's daily rum ration just *after* prayers. ". . . and never," the narrator comments, "were prayers more generally and more punctually attended — so that I thought this method preferable to the punishments inflicted by some military laws for non-attendance on divine service."

Especially in the narrative of the early years, this wide-eyed freshness of perception is perfectly compatible with the young man's shrewdness, and it is nowhere more delightful than in his depiction of the other chief characters in the book. One of the most remarkable qualities in the book is the author's almost total lack of rancor. His brother James, Samuel Keimer, Governor Keith, and General Edward Braddock — all these people may be said to have injured him; yet he presents them all with the charitable curiosity of a man who was once interested in learning from his experience with them something about human nature. I refer here not to the kind of curiosity that can be so easily caricatured, the ingenious Yankee's humor that leads him to tell us how he measured reports of the distance at which the revivalist George Whitefield's voice might be heard. What I mean to admire is the humorous *discovery* of another person's strange faults. Consider the economy of this portrayal of Samuel Keimer, whose faults are balanced against those of the young Franklin:

Keimer and I lived on a pretty good familiar footing and agreed tolerably well, for he suspected nothing of my setting up [for myself]. He retained a great deal of his old enthusiasm and loved argumentation. We therefore had many disputations. I used to work him so with my Socratic method and had trappaned him [that is, tricked him] so often by questions apparently so distant from any point we had in hand, and yet by degrees leading to the point and bringing him into difficulties and contradictions, that at last he grew ridiculously cautious and would hardly answer the most common question without asking first, "What do you intend to infer by that?" However, it gave him so high an opinion of my abilities in the confuting way that he seriously proposed my being his colleague in a project he had of setting up a new sect. He was to preach the doctrines, and I was to confound all opponents. When he came to explain with me upon the doctrines, I found several conundrums which I objected to, unless I might have my way a little, too, and introduce some of mine. Keimer wore his beard at full length, because somewhere in the Mosaic Law it is said, "Thou shalt not mar the corners of thy beard." He likewise kept the seventh day Sabbath, and these two points were essentials with him. I disliked both but agreed to admit them upon condition of his adopting the doctrine of not using animal food. "I doubt," says he, "my constitution will bear it." I assured him it would and that he would be the better for it. He was usually a great glutton, and I wished to give myself some diversion in half-starving him. He consented to try the practice if I would keep him company; I did so, and we held it for three months. Our provisions were purchased, cooked, and brought to us regularly by a woman in the neighbourhood who had from me a list of forty dishes to be prepared for us at different times, in which there entered neither fish, flesh, nor fowl. This whim suited me better at this time from the cheapness of it, not costing us above eighteen pence sterling each per week. I have since kept several Lents most strictly, leaving the common diet for that, and that for common, without the least inconvenience, so that I think there is little in the advice of making those changes by easy gradations. I went on pleasantly, but poor Keimer suffered grievously, tired of the project, longed for the flesh pots of Egypt, and ordered a roast pig. He invited me and two women friends to dine with him, but it being brought too soon upon table, he could not resist the temptation and ate it all up before we came.

Franklin's acute awareness that Keimer is a ridiculously pretentious, affected character does not prevent him from expressing some unsentimental sympathy for his former victim, or from hinting broadly that he himself now disapproves of giving himself diversion at the expense of others—although he might relish the chance to repeat the same experiment. We must remember, in reading this anecdote, that Franklin has previously told us of his decision some years later to abandon the Socratic method, because it had sometimes won him victories that neither he nor his cause deserved. And we must notice that his rational skepticism, his testing by experience, extends even to reason itself.

In an age of reason Franklin was not afraid to admit the limits of reason, nor did he hesitate in his autobiography to illustrate those limits by recounting an experience in which young Franklin himself is the only target of his humor. He used this device on several occasions, but one of them is astonishing in its brilliance, for it not only establishes the author's attitude toward himself but phrases the issue in the key terms of eighteenth-century psychology. The battle in young Franklin is a battle between principle and inclination. The anecdote appears immediately before the vegetarian experiment with Keimer. During a calm on his voyage back from Boston to Philadelphia, Franklin says,

our crew employed themselves catching cod, and hauled up a great number. Till then I had stuck to my resolution to eat nothing that had

had life; and on this occasion I considered . . . the taking every fish as a kind of unprovoked murder, since none of them had or ever could do us any injury that might justify this massacre. All this seemed very reasonable. But I had formerly been a great lover of fish, and when this came hot out of the frying pan, it smelled admirably well. I balanced some time between principle and inclination, till I recollected that when the fish were opened, I saw smaller fish taken out of their stomachs. "Then," thought I, "if you eat one another, I don't see why we mayn't eat you." So I dined upon cod very heartily and have since continued to eat as other people, returning only now and then occasionally to a vegetable diet. So convenient a thing it is to be a *reasonable creature*, since it enables one to find or make a reason for everything one has a mind to do.

Franklin gives us, then, the picture of a relatively innocent, unsophisticated, sometimes foolish young man who confounds or at least survives more sophisticated rivals. Consistently, the young man starts at the level of testing, and he often stumbles onto an important truth. We see his folly and his discoveries through the ironically humorous detachment of a candid old man, whose criticism of the young character's rivals is tempered by the same kind of affectionate tolerance that allows him to see the humor of his own mistakes. The wise old writer expects people to act selfishly, but retains his affection for them. He leads us always to consider major questions in terms of simple practical experience, as when he tells us that he soon gave up converting people to belief in Deism because the result seemed often to be that they thus became less virtuous than before. Deism, he said, might be true, but it did not seem to be very useful. Because he assumed that at best people will usually act according to their conception of their own true interest, because all his experience seemed to confirm this hypothesis, and because metaphysical reasoning often turned out to be erroneous, he concentrated on demonstrating the usefulness of virtue.

It is right here, just at the heart of his most impressive achievement as an autobiographer, that Franklin seems to have made his one great error in communication. Many people, first of all, simply misunderstood him; he did not take sufficient account of the carelessness of readers. Many are completely taken in by the deceptive picture. So effective has Franklin been in demonstrating the usefulness of virtue through repeated anecdotes from his own educational experience, so insistent on effectiveness as a test of what is good in his own life, that many readers simply believe he has no other basis for deciding what is good. They simply conclude that the man who would say, "Honesty is the best *policy*" will be *dis*honest if ever dishonesty becomes the best policy. Readers wonder what the man who tells them candidly that he profited by *appearing* to be humble hopes to gain by *appearing* to be candid.

If I were to follow Franklin and judge chiefly by the results, I would give up trying to clarify the misunderstanding, for I am sure that many readers will refuse to follow me beyond this point. Yet it seems to me important to understand Franklin's intention as clearly as possible, if only to measure properly the degree of his miscalculation or his inadequacy. Let us examine one other brief passage from the *Autobiography,* a statement describing Franklin's own effort to propagate a new set of religious beliefs, to establish a new sect which he proposed, characteristically, to call The Society of the Free and Easy.

In this piece [a book to be called *The Art of Virtue*] it was my design to explain and enforce this doctrine: That vicious actions are not hurtful because they are forbidden, but forbidden because they are hurtful, *the nature of man alone considered;* that it was therefore everyone's interest to be virtuous who wished to be happy *even in this world.*

I have stressed the qualifying phrases in this statement in order to emphasize the nature of Franklin's faith: *the nature of man alone considered;* everyone who wished to be happy *even in this world.* This doctrine of enlightened self-interest represents an important reversal—almost an exact reversal—of a sentence written by a sixteenth-century English Puritan named William Perkins, who in propounding the absolute sovereignty of God had declared: "A thing is not first of all reasonable and just, and then afterwards willed by God; it is first of all willed by God, and thereupon becomes reasonable and just." Yet Franklin's reversal does *not* say that discovering what is apparently to our interest is the only way of *defining* virtue. He, every bit as much as the Calvinist, believes that virtues must be defined by some absolute standard. Vicious actions, he says, *are forbidden*—by the benevolent authority of a wise God and by the universal assent, as he understood it, of wise men throughout history. But some actions *are* inherently vicious, whether or not they seem profitable.

Franklin's faith, then, professes that a true understanding of one's interest even in this world will lead one to virtue. Since the obvious existence of viciousness and folly in every society demonstrates that men do not yet practice the virtues on which most philosophers *have* agreed, finding a way to increase the practice of virtue—the number of virtuous actions—is a sufficiently valuable task to need no elaborate justification. And so the same Franklin who in the year of his death refused to dogmatize on the question of Jesus Christ's divinity because he expected soon to "have an opporunity of knowing the truth with less trouble," contented himself with questions of moral practice. His faith told him that the best way to serve God was to do good to one's fellow men, and he reasoned that just as all wise men preferred benevolent acts to flattery, so the infinitely wise God would not care very much to be flattered, but would prefer to have men *act* benevolently. He denied, however, that any man could ever *deserve* a heavenly, infinite reward for finite actions. He knew perfectly well the implications of his faith, but he saw no reason to worry very much about whether it was absolutely correct. For all his experience indicated that whether or not virtue and interest do coincide, no other argument but that of self-interest will persuade men to act virtuously, and even that argument will not always persuade them.

It is in this context that we must read Franklin's account of the thirteen-week course he gave himself in the Art of Virtue. D. H. Lawrence and other critics have overlooked the humorous self-criticism with which Franklin introduces the account. "It was about this time," Franklin says, "that I conceived the bold and arduous project of arriving at moral perfection. As I knew, or thought I knew, what was right and wrong, I did not see why I might not *always* do the one and avoid the other. But I soon found I had undertaken a task of more difficulty than I had imagined. While my attention was taken up and care employed against one fault, I was often surprised by another." Franklin, you will remember, listed the chief instrumental virtues under thirteen headings and at first devoted a week to concentrating especially on the habit of practicing one of the thirteen virtues. He made himself a chart, and in the daily period that he allotted to meditating the question "What good

have I done today?" he entered a black mark for each action that could be considered a violation of the precepts. He worked to achieve a clear page. At thirteen weeks for each completed "course," he was able, he says, to go through four courses in a year. As he was surprised, at first, to find himself so full of faults, so he was pleased to find that he was able to decrease the number of his faulty actions. He endeavors to persuade us by pointing out that this improvement of conduct made him happier and helped him to prosper. But he makes perfectly clear the relative nature of his progress. He compares his method of attacking one problem at a time to weeding a garden, a task that is never really completed. He tells us not only that he later advanced to taking one course each year (with four weeks for each virtue), but also that he bought a book with ivory pages, so that he could erase the black marks at the end of one term and begin the course anew. The task was endless. Wondering about D. H. Lawrence's reading of Franklin, we may echo his own uncomprehending words: The perfectibility of man, indeed!

In trying to clarify Franklin's beliefs, I have not meant to absolve him of all responsibility for the widespread misunderstanding of his work. As I have already suggested, he invites difficulty by deliberately appearing to be more simple than he is, by choosing the role of the inquisitive, experimental freeman. By daring to reduce metaphysical questions to the terms of practical experience, he sometimes seems to dismiss them entirely, and he draws our attention away from the books that he has read. Thus, although he alludes to the most influential philosophical and psychological treatises of his age, and although he certainly read widely in every kind of learning that attracted his remarkably curious mind, he does not give this theoretical groundwork any important place in the narrative of his life. He mentions that he read John Locke at a certain point, and the Earl of Shaftesbury, and he says that this sort of education is extremely valuable. But in the narrative itself he is plain Benjamin Franklin, asking questions prompted by the situation. Even as he recounts, much later in the book, his successful correspondence with some of the leading scientists of England and the Continent, he underemphasizes his learning and portrays himself as a fortunate and plain, if skillful and talented, amateur.

This effect is reinforced by another quality of Franklin's literary skill, the device of humorous understatement. I have already cited one or two examples, as in his statement about answering the question of the divinity of Jesus. Similarly, he refers to the discovery that an effective preacher was plagiarizing famous English sermons as "an unlucky occurrence," and he says that he preferred good sermons by others to bad ones of the minister's own manufacture. He repeatedly notices ridiculous incongruity by putting an apt word in a startling subordinate place and thus shocking us into a fresh, irreverent look at a subject that we may well have regarded in a conventional way. So he says that for some time he had been regularly absent from Presbyterian church services, "Sunday being my studying day"; and he remarks that enormous multitudes of people admired and respected the revivalist George Whitefield, "notwithstanding his common abuse of them by assuring them they were naturally 'half beasts and half devils.'" This is the method that Henry Thoreau later used in *Walden* when he declared that the new

railroads and highways, which were then called internal improvements, were all external and superficial; it is the method Samuel Clemens employed through his narrator Huckleberry Finn, who says that at mealtime the widow Douglas began by lowering her head and grumbling over the victuals, "though there warn't really anything the matter with them." The device is often delightfully effective in negative argument, in revealing ludicrous inconsistency. But because it depends on an appeal to simple self-reliance, and often to a hard-headed practicality, it is not conducive to the exposition of positive, complex theory. The particular form of Franklin's wit, his decision to portray himself as an inquisitive empiricist, the very success of his effort to exemplify moral values in accounts of practical experience, his doctrine of enlightened self-interest, and the fine simplicity of his exposition — all these combine to make him seem philosophically more naïve, and practically more materialistic, than he is.

Yet this is a great book, and despite the limitations implicit in his pedagogical method, the breadth and richness of Franklin's character do come through to the reasonably careful reader. One chief means, of course, is the urbane yet warm tone of the wise old narrator, who begins by conceding that one of his reasons for writing an autobiographical statement to his son is simply the desire of an old man to talk about himself. We should also notice that although his emotional life is clearly beyond the bounds of his narrative purpose, he expresses an unmistakable affection, even in retrospect, for his parents, his brother, and his wife. His judgment is nowhere firmer or more admirable than in his account of the self-satisfied young Benjamin's return to taunt brother James,

his former master, with the signs of the
Philadelphia journeyman's prosperity.
His record of his wife's life-long usefulness to him is not in the least incom-
patible with genuine affection for her.
And in one brief paragraph citing as
an argument for smallpox vaccination the
death of his own son, "a fine boy of four
years old," he reveals that his serenity
could be rippled by the memory of an
old grief.

We must remember, finally, that Franklin was one of the most beloved men of
his time. The first American who was
called the father of his country, he had
no reason to feel anxious about the quality
of what our own public relations men
would call his "image." He had retired
at the age of 42 to devote the rest of his
long life to public service and scientific
study; he was known internationally as
a faithful patriot who had for decades
defended the popular cause in almost
every political controversy; he had been
a great success at the French court, and
he was a member of the Royal Society in
England. With these sides of his character
known so well, he had no reason to
expect that his instructive *Autobiography*
would be taken as the complete record
of his character, or of his range as a
writer. The polished *Bagatelles* that he
had written in France; the brilliant ironic
essays that he had published in England
during the years just before the Revolution; the state papers that he had written

in all seriousness as an agent of the
Congress—all these formed a part of his
public character before he completed his
work on the *Autobiography*. He could
not foresee that, in a romantic age in
which many writers believed capitalism
and practical science were overwhelming
the human spirit, a novelist like D. H.
Lawrence would make him a symbol of
acquisitive smugness; nor could he foresee that F. Scott Fitzgerald, lamenting in
The Great Gatsby the betrayal of the
great American dream, would couple
Ben Franklin's kind of daily schedule
with a Hopalong Cassidy book, and
would imply that in the 1920's anyone
who followed Franklin's advice would
have to be a stock-waterer or a boot-
legger.

What Franklin represented in his day,
and what we should see in his greatest
book, was something much more complex
than this stereotype. He was deceptively
simple, to be sure; but his life and his
character testified to the promise of
experience, the value of education, the
possibility of uniting fruitful public
service with simple self-reliance, the
profitable conduct of a useful business
enterprise, and the free pursuit of knowledge in both pure and practical science.
His book remains an admirable work of
art, and its author still speaks truth to us
as an admirable representative of the
Enlightenment.

CHARLES AUGUSTIN SAINTE-BEUVE (1804–1869), French man of letters, affectionately wrote of Franklin in his *Portraits of the Eighteenth Century* as a pleasant, honest, comprehending and persuasive utilitarian. Despite Franklin's true stature, however, did he really have an appreciation of the bloom of religion, of chivalry, or of romance? Frenchmen admire Franklin, Saint-Beuve maintains, but why, they wonder, couldn't he be a little more like themselves?*

Charles Augustin Sainte-Beuve

Franklin: "The Most French of Americans"

He embarked on [his] first voyage to England at the close of the year 1724, being then nineteen years of age. He found, on arriving, that the pretended letters of introduction given him by Governor Keith were lures or decoys; in short, he had been hoaxed. He found work in the great printing-office of Palmer, then with Watts, perfected himself in his trade, moralised to his comrades, tried to teach them a better hygiene, a more healthy regimen, and preached to them by example. He met a few men of Letters. When "composing," as a printer, a book on "Natural Religion," by Wollaston, the idea came to him of writing a short metaphysical "Dissertation" to refute some points in the book. This little work,

of which a few copies were printed, brought him into relations with certain freethinking men. In short, during this stay of eighteen months in London he launched himself in more ways than one; he learned from several schools; but especially did he mature quickly in practical knowledge of men and of life.

On leaving Philadelphia he had exchanged promises with Miss Read, whom he expected to marry. One of the errors, the errata of his life, was that soon after his arrival in London he wrote a single letter to this very worthy young girl, telling her that it was improbable he should return to Philadelphia as soon as they had expected. From this indifference it resulted that the young lady,

* From Charles Augustin Sainte-Beuve, *Portraits of the Eighteenth Century* (New York: Frederick Ungar Publishing Co., Inc., 1964), pp. 321–327, 360, 371. Originally published in 1905.

63

urged by her mother, married another man, was very unhappy, and Franklin did not marry her till some years later when, her first marriage being dissolved, she had recovered her liberty.

Here a reflection begins to dawn upon us. An ideal is lacking in this healthy, upright, able, frugal, laborious nature of Franklin—the fine flower of enthusiasm, tenderness, sacrifice,—all that is the dream, and also the charm and the honour of poetic natures. In what I have to say of him I shall not assume to depreciate or belittle him in any way; I simply seek to define him. Let us take him in the matter of love. Young, he feels no irresistible, all-constraining sentiment; he sees Miss Read, she suits him; he conceives both respect and affection for her; but all is subordinate to what is possible and reasonable. Arrived in England, having exchanged promises with her, he begins to doubt whether they can be fulfilled; he tells her so honestly, without otherwise showing much grief. "The fact is," he says, by way of excuse, "the expenses I have had to incur make it impossible for me to pay my passage." Later, when he returns to Philadelphia, with good prospects, and sees Miss Read, sad, melancholy, a widow, or nearly so, he returns to her; but not until he has himself missed another marriage, and because he thinks the state of celibacy full of vices and inconveniences. "Marriage, after all," he says, "is the natural state of man. An unmarried man is not a complete human being: he resembles one-half of a pair of scissors without its other half, and consequently, is not even half as useful as if the two were put together."

He tries to correct his first mistake and succeeds. Married at twenty-four years of age; he finds in his wife for many years a tender and faithful companion, who aids him much in the work of his shop. That is his ideal: do not ask more of him. When he is old and in Paris, he spends a day at Auteuil, talking nonsense with Mme. Helvétius; telling her he wished to marry her and that she was very foolish to resolve to be faithful to her late husband, the philosopher. The next morning he writes a very pretty letter to her, in which he pretends that he has been transported in a dream to the Elysian Fields; where he finds Helvétius in person, who has married again, and is much astonished to hear that his former wife on earth persists in being faithful to his memory. While he talks very pleasantly with Franklin, in comes the new Mme. Helvétius, bringing coffee which she has prepared with her own hands:

"Instantly," writes the lively old man, "I recognised her as Madame Franklin, my former American wife. I claimed her; but she said, coldly: 'I was your good wife for forty-nine years and four months, almost half a century; be satisfied with that. I have formed here a new connection which will last through eternity.'—Displeased with this refusal of my Eurydice, I at once resolved to quit those thankless shades and return to this good world to see the sun and you. Here I am; let us avenge ourselves."

All that is gay, a pretty, piquant, social jest, but the lack of sentiment reveals itself.

Also, there is a flower, a bloom, of religion, of honour, of chivalry, which we must not ask of Franklin. He is not obliged to comprehend chivalry, and he gives himself no trouble to do so. When the founding of the Society of the Cincinnati is in question, he opposes it with good reasons, but he makes no reservation in favour of chivalry, considered historically and in the past. He forgets Lord Falkland, that perfect result of delicate and gallant chivalry grafted upon ancient loyalty. He applies to the examination of chivalry a method of moral arithmetic which he is fond of employing, and starting from the principle that "a son derives only half from the family of his father, the other half from that of his mother," he proves by figures that in nine generations (supposing a pure, intact genealogy) there remains in the person who inherits the title of "Knight" only the five-hundred-dozenth part of the original knight or noble. He brings everything down to arithmetic and strict reality, assigning no part to human imagination.

So with religion. He returns to it, after his early freethinking, in a sincere and touching manner. I know no deist who shows a more living sense of faith than Franklin; he seems to believe, on all occasions, in a Providence actually present and perceptible. But there again, what was it that most contributed to bring him back to religion? It was seeing that, during the time when he was decidedly a sceptic, he failed in fidelity to a trust, and that two or three other sceptics of his acquaintance allowed themselves to do him certain wrongs involving money and integrity. "I began to suspect," he says, "that these doctrines, though they may be true, are not very profitable." Thus he returns to religion through utility. The useful is always, and preferably, his measure.

Franklin is by nature above all the anxieties of a Childe-Harold, all the susceptibilities of a Chateaubriand. We, of the hasty and vivacious French race, would like him to have had a little of ourselves in him. The devotion of a Chevalier d'Assas, the passion of a Chevalier Des Grieux, the folly of Parisina or Ariel, all that is in our thoughts, and we feel that the wings to soar are lacking, at any rate in youth, when a man

cannot pass at will from one of these worlds to the other. Nevertheless, let us see Franklin just as he was in his moral beauty, and in his true stature. That judicious, firm, shrewd, comprehending, honest man will be unshaken, immovable, when injustice assails him and his compatriots. He will also do all in his power, for years, with the mother-country, to enlighten opinion, and prevent extreme measures; until the last instant he will strive to bring about a reconciliation founded on equity. One day when a man of great influence in England, Lord Howe, gave him hopes (on the very eve of the rupture), a tear of joy rolled down his cheek; but when injustice hardened itself and an obstinate pride plugged its ears, then the purest and most invincible of passions swept him along, and he who thought that "all peace is good and all war evil" was for war then, for the holy war of a legitimate and patriotic defence.

In the ordinary current of his life Franklin is ever the most gracious, smiling, and persuasive of utilitarians. "I approve, for my part, that people should amuse themselves now and then with poesy," he says, "as much as is needed to perfect their style; but not beyond that." Yet he himself, without being aware of it, has a form of imagination and a way of saying things that make him not only the philosopher, but sometimes the poet of common sense. In a little Diary of travel, written at the age of twenty (1726) during his return from London to Philadelphia, speaking of I know not what atrocious description that was given him of a former Governor of the Isle of Wight, he says:

"What surprised me was that the old fellow of a porter spoke to me of the governor with a perfect notion of his character. In a word, I believe it to be impossible that a man, had he the craft of a devil, can live and die a wretch and yet conceal it so well that he could take with him to the grave the reputation of an honourable man. It will always happen that, by one accident or another, he is unmasked. Truth and sincerity have a certain natural and distinctive lustre which can never be counterfeited; they are like fire and flame, no one can paint them."

Pointing out a method of economy that would ensure having money at all times in our pocket—a method that consists (independently of the fundamental counsel of work and honesty) in "spending always a penny less than the net profit," he adds:

"In that way thy flat pocket will begin to swell and will no longer cry out that its belly is empty. Thou wilt not be insulted by thy creditors or harassed by want, gnawed by hunger, or numbed by nakedness. The whole horizon will shine brighter to thine eyes, and pleasure will gush from the innermost recesses of thy heart."

If ever the doctrine of economy came into the world with contentment and mirth and a sort of familiar poesy of expression, we must look for it in Franklin. An inward warmth of feeling animates his prudence; a ray of sun lights up and cheers his honesty.

Franklin returned to Philadelphia from his first journey to England in 1726; and, after a few attempts, he established himself as a printer at twenty-one years of age, first with a partner, but soon alone. He makes a sort of moral inventory of himself at this decisive moment of his life. He enumerates his principles, from which he never afterwards departed. "I was convinced that *truth, sincerity,* and *integrity* in the relations between men are of the first importance for the happiness of life, and I formed the written resolution, which is always placed in my Diary-book, to practise them as long as

I live." To this real and fundamental probity, Franklin took pains to add the legitimate social profit that accrued from it. But, while observing the constant little cares that he gave and the minute pains he took to make himself more and more virtuous within, and more and more considered without we must never separate in him the appearance from the reality. He was, if you will, the shrewdest and most prudent of honest men, but also the least hypocritical.

* * *

When he quitted France, in July, 1785, Franklin was wholly one of us; he repaid us the hospitality he had received and for the popularity by which he was surrounded, from the first to the last day, by feelings of affection and reciprocal esteem. We may say of him that he was the most French of Americans.

I insist upon this point because to detach such or such a passage from his letters, without distinguishing the times at which they were written, might lead us to infer quite the contrary. In politics, I cannot follow the progress of his negotiations in the complicated circumstances through which he led them; such an analysis would require a long chapter. I shall insist only on this one important point: Franklin was in no way ungrateful towards France. From the moment that the treaty of alliance was concluded, he had but one answer to all the overtures made to him to listen to proposals from England: "We cannot negotiate without France." America had been a submissive daughter until the day when she emancipated herself from England, but in vain did the latter secretly recall her and endeavour to tempt her in underhand ways; America was now a faithful spouse. Such was the principle that Franklin professed on all occasions, public or private; and it drew upon him in America the reputation of being too French. But he believed, contrary to his distinguished colleagues (such as Mr. Adams), that Americans could not express too openly their feelings of gratitude to France, and to her young and virtuous king. . . .

* * *

If all those who had conversed with Franklin at Passy had truly understood his precepts and his measures, they would have thought twice before undertaking in the Old World a universal recasting. At the same time, I must add (even if some contradiction be found in it) that it was difficult for those who listened to him not to take fire, not to be tempted to reform society radically; for he was himself, in his general way of thinking and presenting matters, a great, too great a simplifier. This practical man had nothing in him that discouraged a Utopia; on the contrary, he rather invited it by the novelties and facilities of the outlook he opened towards the future. He gave, in talking, a desire to apply his ideas, but he did not give in equal measure to those who listened to him (the Condorcets and the Chamforts, for instance,) his temperament, his discretion in details, and his prudence. . . .

CHARLES ANGOFF (b. 1902), editor, literary critic, and former New York University professor of English, maintains that we have placed Franklin on too high a pedestal. He had an excellent mind but was annoyed by abstract ideas except those of the corner grocery store. The importance of his scientific studies has been exaggerated and his political achievements have been overrated. As to his writings, his style may be clear, but many of his ideas were borrowed from others and what he left us is often vulgar and superficial. Franklin was popular, although he could never be considered a great man. To what extent do Angoff and D. H. Lawrence agree on Franklin's shortcomings?*

Charles Angoff

Franklin: A Colonial Lowbrow

Franklin made a relatively small contribution to the American argument during the Revolutionary period. He exerted a powerful influence, but it was "chiefly through the customary channels of diplomacy, and in a voluminous correspondence with friends and public men on both sides of the Atlantic; and his contemporary publications, comparatively few in number, carried weight because of their directness and sturdy common sense, and of the fame of their writer" rather than because of their intrinsic merit. He never knew precisely what all the noise was about, and the philosophical and theological pamphlets of such men as Mayhew, Cooper, Otis, and Lee always left him somewhat puzzled. Indeed, so doubtful was he of the principles involved that more than once he came pretty close to allying himself with the loyalists. But on each occasion luck was with him, and he chose the right side.

He was the first great fixer of American political history, and also, if John Adams is to be believed, its first great trimmer. He made friends of the English, he made friends of the French, he made friends of the Germans, he made friends of the Federalists, he made friends of the Republicans, and when he died the whole civilized world mourned him. Just where he stood on any one of the fundamental issues is still something of a mystery. He trusted the people, and he didn't

---

*From Charles Angoff, *A Literary History of the American People,* Vol. II, (New York: Alfred A. Knopf, Inc., 1931), pp. 295–310. Footnotes omitted.

trust them. He claimed to be a deist, but he contributed to all the churches in his neighborhood, and believed in the transmigration of souls. All his life long he preached a copy-book morality, but he himself was extremely careless in his personal affairs. He spent money lavishly, ate so much that he suffered from gout for years and years, and when he was married at the age of twenty-four brought to his wife, as a wedding present, an illegitimate son.

He wrote a great deal, but it was chiefly to make money, or to forget the pain of his gout. He knew his public well. He made a fortune as a newspaper and a magazine editor, and his "Poor Richard's Almanac" was an immediate success: it sold 10,000 copies within the first three months of publication. He did not produce one truly great work of the imagination, and his general style was surely not above the ordinary, but his work achieved an amazing popularity.

All this was probably a colossal misfortune to the United States, for, despite his good fellowship and occasional good sense, Franklin represented the least praiseworthy qualities of the inhabitants of the New World: miserliness, fanatical practicality, and lack of interest in what are usually known as spiritual things. Babbittry was not a new thing in America, but he made a religion of it, and by his tremendous success with it he grafted it upon the American people so securely that the national genius is still suffering from it. He extolled the virtues of honesty, industry, chastity, cleanliness, and temperance—all excellent things. But it never occurred to him that with these alone life is not worth a fool's second thought. Philosophy, poetry, and the arts spring from different sources.

Franklin was born in Boston on January 17, 1706. At the age of ten he was taken from school to assist his father, a tallow chandler and soap-boiler by trade. Three years later he was apprenticed to his older brother James, editor and publisher of the *New England Courant*. He began his career as a writer by slipping under the door of his brother's printing office an anonymous contribution, which was accepted. He was unable to get along with James, so in 1723 he ran away from Boston, first to New York, then to Philadelphia, where he found work in the printing office of one Samuel Keimer, a Jew. The following year he went to London to get type to open an office of his own, but instead he spent the next two years in drinking and whoring. In 1726 he was penniless, so he returned to Philadelphia, where he opened a shop of his own, in which he did a great deal of the public printing of Pennsylvania, Delaware, and New Jersey. In 1728 he formed the Junto Club for group reading and debating, and for the purpose of helping reform the world.

In 1729 he bought from Keimer the *Universal Instructor in All Arts and Sciences and Pennsylvania Gazette,* which at the time had a subscription list of not more than 90. The paper in time became the leading public print between New York and Charleston. He wrote a number of essays for it, including "A Meditation on a Quart Mug," "Dialogue Between Philocles and Horatio Concerning Virtue and Pleasure," and "A Witch Trial at Mount Holly." About this time he also wrote the pamphlet, "A Modest Inquiry into the Nature and Necessity of Paper Currency." The argument in it was a wholly false one, but it got Franklin the job of printing most of the worthless paper money of Pennsylvania.

In 1732 he began the publication of "Poor Richard's Almanac," which for twenty-five years was one of the most popular publications in the Colonies. Its average annual sale was more than 10,000 copies. In the same year he established in Philadelphia the first circulating library in America. In 1730 he married Deborah Read of Philadelphia. She died in 1774. In 1741 he began the second monthly publication in America, the *General Magazine and Historical Chronicle for All the British Colonies in America,* which died with the sixth number.

1732

Franklin had very little schooling in his youth, but he made up for it by omnivorous reading. While still in his teens he read Plutarch, Bunyan, Defoe, Mather, Locke, Collins, Hume, and Shaftesbury. He early became interested in scientific matters, and kept that interest up till his dying day. Nothing was alien to his experimental mind. He was in the habit of writing about his experiments and general ideas to scientists and philosophers in Europe, and thus he earned the respect of many of them. He in this way became the friend, in England, of Collinson, Priestley, Price, Hume, Adam Smith, Robertson, Lord Kames, Mandeville, Joseph Banks, Bishop Watson, Burke, Chatham, and Lord Shelburne; and in France, of Turgot, Mirabeau, Quesnay, La Rochefoucauld, Lafayette, Vergennes, Condorcet, Buffon, Voltaire, Robespierre, Lavoisier, and D'Alembert. His electrical experiments he used to report in the form of letters to the English physicist, Peter Collinson, who later published all of them in London in 1751 under the title, "Experiments and Observations in Electricity, Made at Philadelphia in America, by Mr. Benjamin Franklin." The following year Franklin showed the identity of lightning and electricity by his famous kite experiment, and he invented the lightning rod at the same time.

He began his active political life in 1736, when he was chosen clerk of the General Assembly of Pennsylvania; he retained the office till 1750. In 1737 he was made postmaster of the Colony. About the same time he organized a night watch, a fire company, the American Philosophical Society, and a sort of high high-school, which in 1779 became the University of Pennsylvania. In 1751 he helped establish a hospital in Philadelphia. By this time, because of his scientific discoveries, he had an international reputation, and was the foremost individual man in the Colonies. Harvard, Yale, Oxford and St. Andrews gave him honorary degrees. He was elected a Fellow of the Royal Society, and was one of the eight foreign associates of the French Academy of Science. So great was his renown then that Lord Jeffrey, editor of the *Edinburgh Review,* said of him. "In one point of view the name of Franklin must be considered as standing higher than any of the others which illustrated the Eighteenth Century. Distinguished as a statesman he was equally great as a philosopher, thus uniting in himself a rare degree of excellence in both these pursuits, to excel in either of which is deemed the highest praise."

He was a member of the Colonial Congress held in Albany in 1754, at which he submitted a plan for colonial union. The Congress adopted the plan, but it was rejected by the colonial assemblies. In 1759 he wrote "An Historical Review of the Constitution and Government of Pennsylvania," and then went to England as a representative of the Province. He returned to America in 1762, and in 1763 traveled in all the Colonies inspecting the postal service in each. He worked mightily against the Stamp Act, but when it was finally passed by Parliament he thought it would be enforced, and he suggested his friend John Hughes as stamp distributor of Pennsylvania. This was a great political blunder, and for the rest of his days it was brought up against him by his enemies. In 1766 he went to England again, and appeared at the bar of the House of Commons to answer questions in regard to the situation in America. In the political discussions at home in the next eight years he contributed several articles to the newspapers, but he was not one of the leaders. His course was too moderate for the extremists in either country. Nobody really knew precisely where he stood, so evasive was he. He kept up this caution even after he signed the Declaration of Independence, and it was largely on account of the lack of definiteness in his political opinions that John Adams, in a letter to his cousin, Samuel Adams dated December 7, 1778, said of him:

He loves his Ease, hates to offend, and seldom gives any opinion till obliged to do it. . . . You know that, although he has as determined a soul as any man, yet it is his constant Policy never to say "yes" or "no" decidedly but when he cannot avoid it.

Nevertheless, he managed to win back the confidence of the people at large after the Revolution, and in 1776 he was made president of the Constitutional Convention of Pennsylvania. In the same year he was chosen as envoy to France, where he showed great skill as a negotiator. He was also a great success socially. He was the star attraction in the salons of Mmes. Helvetius and Brillon. He set up a printing press of his own in Passy, and there printed a collection of writings since known as "The Bagatelles." They included "The Ephemera," "The Morals of Chess," "The Whistle," and "The Dialogue Between Franklin and the Gout." They were all written between 1778 and 1785 for the amusement of his friends in Paris. They were not a new literary form for him. In 1773 he published in the *Gentleman's Magazine* two similar things: "An Edict by the King of Prussia" and "Rules by which A Great Empire May Be Reduced to A Small One." Stuart P. Sherman, in a burst of enthusiasm, called them masterpieces of irony, adding that "Swift might have been pleased to sign" them.

On his return to this country in 1785 he took part in the debates of the Constitutional Convention, but it was hardly a prominent part. Franklin was very good in organizing post offices and fire departments, but he was completely lost when it came to drafting organic bodies of laws. Basic philosophical ideas were beyond him. He did not approve of the new Constitution, but he regarded it as the best obtainable and therefore signed it. His last act was the signing of an anti-slavery petition to Congress as president of the Pennsylvania Society for Promoting the Abolition of Slavery. He died in Philadelphia on April 17, 1790, at the age of eighty-four.

One American critic has said, "Intellectually there are few men who are Franklin's peers in all the ages and nations." This opinion must be put down as an amiable exaggeration. Franklin had an excellent mind, but surely he was not a philosopher. Abstract ideas, save those of the corner grocery store, somehow irked him. He was not an original thinker, but he was one of the best eclectic thinkers who ever lived. He lived in an age of rationalism, and few other men of that time were so imbued with the ideas then afloat. The current French philosophy was in large part precisely to his taste. "In their youth, Voltaire and Franklin had both drunk at the same spring: the English radicalism of Gordon, Collins, and Shaftesbury. But Voltaire had developed it into a witty, dry and sharp-tongued philosophy, while Franklin had expanded it with good fellowship and sentimentality."

This good fellowship of his explains his strange brand of deism. He was not a believer, but there were many reservations to his unbelief. In Paris he refused to have any priests around him, and this caused much surprise in a land where every diplomat had his private chaplain. He told everybody that he could say his prayers himself. "He considered the Church of Rome to be like raw sugar, the American churches like refined sugar, for they were less influenced by hierarchical systems or mysticism. He saw a certain advantage in the multiplicity of churches in the world, as that made for competition and competition made for trade, but he didn't think churches were of any importance in Heaven." He spoke of miracles with levity, but he had some belief in Pythagoreanism. In other words he was pretty much confused about the whole business. His main contribution to the religious question was little more than a good-natured tolerance influenced largely by his shrewd business sense. Nobody but Franklin could have reconciled deism with the practice of contributing money to all the denominations in Philadelphia.

On the few occasions when he tried to be philosophical about religion he made a sorry spectacle, as in the following celebrated letter to Dr. Ezra Stiles, president of Yale. The letter is dated March 9, 1790—a little more than a month before Franklin's death.

You desire to know something of my Religion. It is the first time that I have been questioned upon it. But I do not take your curiosity amiss, & shall endeavor in a few words to gratify it. Here is my Creed. I believe in one God, Creator of the Universe: That he governs the World by his Providence. That he ought to be worshipped. That the most acceptable service we can render to him, is doing good to his other Children. That the Soul of Man is immortal, and will be treated with Justice in another Life, respect^g its Conduct in this. These I take to be the fundamental Principles of all sound Religion, and I regard them as you do, in whatever Sect I meet with them. As to *Jesus of Nazareth,* my Opinion of whom you particularly desire, I think the *System of Morals & his Religion as he left them to us, the best the World ever saw;* but I apprehend it has received various corrupting changes; and I have, with most of the present Dissenters in Engld, some Doubts as to his Divinity: tho' it is a question I do not dogmatize upon, hav^g never studied it, & think it needless to busy myself with it now, when I expect soon an Opport^y of know^g the Truth with less Trouble. I see no harm however in its being believed, if that Belief has the good Consequence, as probably it has, of mak^g his Doctrines more respected & better observed, esp^y as I do not perceive that the Supreme [Being] takes it amiss, by distinguish^g the Believers, in his Gov^t of the World, with any particular Marks of his Displeasure. I shall only add respect^g myself, that hav^g experienced the Goodness of that Being in conducting me prosperously thro' a long Life, I have no doubt of its Continuance in the next, tho' without the smallest Conceit of meriting such Goodness.

Try to imagine Thomas Paine dismissing God and the churches in so flippant a way!

Franklin's most popular work was, and still is, his "Autobiography." It was the longest of his writings, and the one he did most carelessly. He wrote it whenever he felt like it, and apparently cared very little if it was ever published. The greater part of it he composed while he was in England as agent for the United Colonies. Parts of it were printed in France between 1791 and 1798, but the complete "Autobiography" did not appear till 1868 under the editorship of John Bigelow, who copied it from the original MS., which he obtained in France.

John Bach McMaster the historian has called the book the greatest biographical work of any kind ever written in America, and has compared it to Defoe's "Robinson Crusoe" in literary merit. The book is very simply written, and is quite readable. But it is lacking in almost everything else necessary to a really great work of *belles lettres:* grace of expression, charm of personality, and intellectual flight. The essential commonplaceness of the man is in every line of it. He was incapable of dreaming, of doubting, of being mystified. The only mysteries he understood were those that lent themselves easily to experimentation. The mysteries of poetry, of philosophy, and even of religion were beyond him. Doing good, making money, and gaining the approbation of one's fellows were the only things that occupied him when addressing the public. Witness his "Scheme for Aiming at Moral Perfection. . . ."

Not a word about nobility, not a word about honor, not a word about grandeur of soul, not a word about charity of mind! Carlyle called Franklin the father of all the Yankees. That was a libel against the tribe, for the Yankees have produced Thoreau, Hawthorne, and Emily Dickinson. It would be more accurate to call Franklin the father of all the Kiwanians.

Franklin began his "Poor Richard's Almanac" in December, 1732. It was an imitation of the English "Poor Robin's Almanac." It attained a great popularity at once. "Three editions were sold within the month of its appearance. The average sale for twenty-five years was 10,000 a year. He was sometimes obliged to put it to press in October to get a supply of copies to the remote Colonies by the beginning of the year. It has been translated into nearly if not quite every written language, and several different translations of it have been made into the French and German." The most celebrated number was that for the year 1757, the last Franklin edited. It contained the well-known speech on thrift, called "Father Abraham's Speech at an Auction," which was reprinted many times as "The Way of Wealth." For some time it was used as a text in the French schools, under the title of "La Science du Bonhommie Richard. . . ."

Bigelow thinks that "Poor Richard" contains "some of the best fun as well as the wisest counsel that ever emanated from Franklin's pen." That is quite true, but absolutely considered the wisdom is of a low order. It points downward. True enough, it was addressed to the common man, but one does not always have to be a vulgarian when talking to the man in the street. Consider Jesus and Socrates and Confucius and Lao-Tze. Consider Montaigne. Consider even Krylov. . . .

Of "The Bagatelles," which Franklin wrote while he was in France, little more can be said than for "Poor Richard." Even after more than ten years of Parisian salon life he could not forget his twopenny philosophy. Mme. Brillon fell in love with him, and carried on a long correspondence with him, some of which he published on his private press in Passy. How did Franklin repay her for her eager caresses and elegant dinners? He wrote her a little story, entitled "The Whistle," the moral of which was that one must always be careful not to spend too much money on trifles! She had sent him a description of what she would like to find in Paradise, and Franklin answered thus:

I am charmed with your description of Paradise, and with your plan of living there; and I approve much of your conclusion, that, in the mean time, we should draw all the good we can from this world. In my opinion, we might all draw more good from it than we do, and suffer less evil, if we would take care not to give too much for *whistles.* For to me it seems, that most of the unhappy people we meet with, are become so by neglect of that caution.

You ask what I mean? You love stories, and will excuse my telling one of myself.

When I was a child of seven years old, my friends, on a holiday, filled my pockets with coppers. I went directly to a shop where they sold toys for children; and, being charmed with the sound of a *whistle,* that I met by the way in the hands of another boy, I voluntarily offered and gave all my money for one. I then came home, and went whistling all over the house, much pleased with my *whistle,* but disturbing all the family. My brothers, and sisters, and cousins, understanding the bargain I had made, told me I had given four times as much for it as it was worth; put me in mind of what good things I might have bought with the rest of the money; and laughed at me so much for my folly, that I cried with vexation; and the reflection gave me more chagrin than the *whistle* gave me pleasure.

This however was afterwards of use to me, the impression continuing in my mind; so that often, when I was tempted to buy some unnecessary thing, I said to myself, *Don't give too much for the whistle;* and I saved my money.

Franklin perpetrated one more piece of literature that has somehow escaped the literary historians, but that surely deserves mention. That was his proposed new version of the Bible. Like the immortal authors of the Bay Psalm Book he did not like the King James version. He said:

It is now more than one hundred and seventy years since the translation of our common English Bible. The language in that time is

much changed, and the style being obsolete, and thence less agreeable, is perhaps one reason why the reading of that excellent book is of late so much neglected. I have therefore thought it well to procure a new version in which, preserving the sense, the turn of phrase and manner of expression should be modern. I do not pretend to have the necessary abilities for such a work myself; I throw out the hint for the consideration of the learned.

The following was his idea of how the first chapter of Job should read:

Verse 6. *King James version.*—Now there was a day when the sons of God came to present themselves before the Lord, and Satan came also amongst them.

Verse 6. *New version by Franklin.*—And it being *levee* day in heaven, all God's nobility came to court, to present themselves before him; and Satan also appeared in the circle, as one of the ministry.

Verse 7. *King James version.*—And the Lord said unto Satan: Whence comest thou? Then Satan answered the Lord, and said: From going to and fro in the earth, and from walking up and down in it.

Verse 7. *New version by Franklin.*—And God said to Satan: you have been some time absent; where were you? And Satan answered: I have been at my country-seat, and in different places visiting my friends.

Verse 8. *King James version.*—And the Lord said unto Satan: Hast thou considered my servant Job, that there is none like him in the earth, a perfect and an upright man, one that feareth God, and escheweth evil?

Verse 8. *New version by Franklin.*—And God said: Well, what do you think of Lord Job? You see he is my best friend, a perfectly honest man, full of respect for me, and avoiding everything that might offend me. . . .

This crime against beautiful letters was in perfect keeping with Franklin's general character. He had a cheap and shabby soul, and the upper levels of the mind were far beyond his reach. His one attempt at dignified philosophical speculation, "Dissertation on Liberty and

Necessity" (1725), was so bad that even he was later ashamed of it. As for his scientific experiments, they have been vastly overrated. "All that he invented was current supposition at the time; his work was rather in confirming and defining the scientific notions of others."

His writings enjoyed a vast popularity in his own day, and still do in ours, but that should not blind us to their inferior quality. All he had to say he borrowed from others, and what is worse, he was a bad borrower. The literature of England in the Seventeenth and Eighteenth Centuries was the most glorious in its entire history. There was the immortal King James version of the Bible, and there was the galaxy of stars beginning with Shakespeare and ending with Pope. Franklin read them all, but when he came to imitate and to borrow did he choose any of these? He rejected the entire lot, and instead picked "Poor Robin's Almanac"! And of the King James version his chief comment was that its style was "obsolete"!

To call Franklin "one of the greatest masters of English expression" is the veriest nonsense. Almost any one of the Eighteenth Century New England theologians wrote better. Franklin, to be sure, was easier to understand, but there was far less in him worth understanding. His influence on the national letters, in the long run, was probably nil. "He founded no school of literature. He gave no impetus to letters. He put his name to no great work of history, of poetry, of fiction."

But by his international prominence and by the wide circulation of his twopenny philosophy he left a lasting impression on the national culture. In him "the 'lowbrow' point of view for the first time took definite shape, stayed itself with axioms, and found a sanction in the idea of 'policy.'" Thrift, industry, and determination were essential virtues in the building of the nation, but they were not, then or at any other time in history, of sufficient human dignity to build a life philosophy on. Franklin did precisely that for his private life, and by the force of his personality did more than any other man in his day to graft it upon the American people. The vulgarity he spread is still with us.

PHILIP GLEASON (b. 1927), who teaches history at
the University of Notre Dame, reveals in this essay
the antagonisms that led to Franklin's defeat as a
candidate for the Pennsylvania Assembly in the election
of 1764. When Franklin sided with Quaker leaders in
advocating that Pennsylvania be made a royal colony,
he came under heavy attack. The generally favorable
image of Franklin was all but abandoned in the heat
of the controversy. Franklin's final defeat was in part
due to the hostility of the Pennsylvania Germans, who
resented his calling them *"Palatine Boors."* How was
Franklin accused of plotting and sedition? How were
his scientific achievements ridiculed? And how was
his personal morality and integrity held up to
question?*

Philip Gleason

Franklin and the Election of 1764

Recent investigations have shown not
only that Benjamin Franklin is a key
figure in understanding colonial and
Revolutionary America, but also that
the study of his posthumous influence
and reputation offers fruitful insights
into the development of the American
mind. Over a decade ago "Franklin's
Legacy to the Gilded Age" was duly
recorded, and more recently two studies
have explored the "Franklin Image"
in the popular national consciousness
and his stature as an American hero.
Another scholar has demonstrated that
F. Scott Fitzgerald tried to link his Gatsby
more closely to the American tradition
by patterning Gatsby's youthful resolutions after the famous regimen outlined
in the *Autobiography*. Less has been
done, however, to discover Franklin's
standing among his colonial contemporaries, especially in the pre-Revolu-
tionary period. John Adams's rather
grumpy judgments are well known, but
from a later date; and Franklin's lioniza-
tion in France is likewise irrelevant to
his stature in colonial America. This
article focuses on a restricted, but highly
charged, moment in Franklin's colonial
experience in an attempt to amend the
neglect of his earlier reputation and to
suggest reasons for some of the currents
of derogatory opinion about Franklin
which persisted all through the nineteenth century.

A strong tincture of aristocratic con-

*From Philip Gleason, "A Scurrilous Colonial Election and Franklin's Reputation," *William and Mary
Quarterly*, Vol. XVIII, No. 1 (January, 1961), pp. 68–84. Footnotes omitted.

tempt for Franklin is one of the most striking things revealed by studies of his reputation. Early in the nineteenth century, Joseph Dennie, a Philadelphia editor whose ideal for American literature and culture was patrician gentility, castigated Franklin for the unoriginality of his writing, the impurity of his life, and the unsoundness of his religion. In the 1890's it was reported that bitter feeling toward the man they called the "old rogue" still survived "among some of the descendants of the people of his time, and fifty or sixty years ago there were virtuous old ladies living in Philadelphia who would flame into indignation at the mention of his name." Matrons of the City of Brotherly Love insured their gentility in 1895 by refusing membership in the Colonial Dames to Franklin's great-great-granddaughter, and shortly thereafter a speaker at the dedication of his statue noted: "Time was when in Philadelphia it was not 'fashionable' to visit Franklin. Time *is* when in a small and ever decreasing circle it *is* not fashionable to praise him."

This upper-class distaste for Franklin had its origin in his own time, and much of its rancor can be traced to the Pennsylvania election of 1764, in which Franklin led the opposition to the "Proprietary or Gentlemen's party, as it was sometimes called." One of Franklin's principal antagonists in this contest was the Reverend William Smith, an Anglican clergyman who was provost of the Philadelphia College, and the continuity of anti-Franklin feeling is suggested by the later conduct of the Smith family. On Franklin's death, Smith was called upon as a former friend and close associate of Franklin to deliver a eulogy to his memory; Smith downed his natural impulses and did so, but his heart was not in his work. A "family tradition" has

it that Smith's daughter said to him, "I don't think you believed more than one tenth part of what you said of Old Ben Lightning Rod." Smith made no response, but in the 1880's a descendant of his had considerably more to say. This later Smith abused Franklin in his biography of William Smith and circulated privately among his friends the vicious description of Franklin as atheist, fornicator, and hypocrite, which originally had been made by William Cobbett in "The Life of Peter Porcupine."

Franklin himself realized what enduring animosities had been aroused by the political wars of 1764. "You know," he wrote to his daughter a month after the election, "I have many enemies, all indeed on the public account, (for I cannot recollect that I have in a private capacity given just cause of offence to any one whatever,) yet they are enemies, and very bitter ones. . . ." Franklin was, of course, a famous man already, but he enjoyed before the tumults of 1764 a more uniform respect than was the case later. In January 1763 a Pennsylvania Assemblyman recorded his pleasure at meeting Franklin: "A Gentleman, whose Patriotic Zeal & assiduous Exertion of his Superior talents in the service of his Country, had render'd him Equally famous & universally beloved and Esteem'd." But the bitterness engendered by the election campaign affected Franklin's standing so adversely that John Dickinson, one of his more moderate opponents, could aver on the floor of the Assembly "that no man in Pennsylvania is at this time so much the object of the public dislike, as he that has been mentioned [Franklin]." Dickinson declined to elaborate on the "surprising height" to which the hatred of Franklin was carried, but an examination of the anti-Franklin feeling of 1764 is helpful in accounting for the later vicissitudes of his reputation.

According to a contemporary observer, the election of representatives to the Pennsylvania Assembly in 1764 "was, perhaps, the warmest that ever was held in this province. . . ." A number of factors contributed to this heat. For years the customary friction between colonial assemblies and colonial governors had been exacerbated in Pennsylvania by quarrels over the taxation of land owned by the Proprietors: the Assembly insisted on trying to tax the land but the proprietary governors were under instructions from the Penns to resist taxation. The principal issue in the 1764 election was whether Pennsylvania should retain its proprietary government, or whether it should be brought directly under the Crown as a royal colony. The majority of the Assembly, controlled by the Quaker Party, favored changing the government, while the "New Ticket" in the election was friendly to the Proprietors and opposed to the Quakers.

Religious antagonisms were added to the constitutional question when the Presbyterians supported the proprietary government. This came about not so much because the Presbyterians were fond of the Proprietors, but because the urban-centered oligarchy in the Assembly was Quaker and the back-country minority was Presbyterian. Three Quaker-dominated counties around Philadelphia had twenty-four of the Assembly's thirty-six seats, while five outlying counties in which the Scots-Irish Presbyterians were the politically active element had only ten seats. Not only did the back-country Presbyterians resent their under-representation, they were aroused to fury by the Indian policy pursued by the Quaker majority. Quaker pacifism and

humanitarianism seemed to them incomprehensible in the face of repeated atrocities during the French and Indian War and Pontiac's Rebellion; the frontiersmen accused the Quakers of wishing to sacrifice them in order to preserve profitable trade relations with the Indians. The Assembly maintained that the Proprietors' refusal to bear their fair share of the burden of taxation was the obstacle to adequate frontier defense, but many of Philadelphia's disfranchised "meaner sort," as well as the city's Presbyterians, sympathized with the back-country men against the despised Quaker oligarchy.

The crisis that sparked the attempt to eliminate proprietary government was provided by the outbreak of the Paxton Boys in December 1763. These back-country hotheads, driven to undiscriminating fury by Indian depredations, fell upon and murdered a group of peaceful Indians, long allied to the province, at Conestoga and later at Lancaster. When a group of Moravian Indians was brought to Philadelphia for protection, a large number of back-country men marched on the city itself to enforce their demands upon the Assembly, or, it was alleged, to destroy these Indians too. A civil war threatened for a time, as even Quakers prepared to resist the marchers; further violence was averted when Franklin and three others met the insurgents at Germantown and persuaded them to disperse, assuring them that their grievances would be taken up by the Assembly. But frontier defense was again stymied by a wrangle between the Assembly and the governor over the taxation of proprietary lands and control of the militia.

Franklin had long felt that removing the proprietary government and making Pennsylvania a royal colony was the only solution for the problem, and this seemed an opportune moment for the attempt. On March 24, 1764, the Assembly adopted a series of resolutions against the Proprietors which had been introduced by Joseph Galloway, Franklin's chief lieutenant, and adjourned to consult the people on the question of changing the provincial government. Petitions and counter-petitions were gathered, parliamentary battling ensued in the next session of the Assembly, the change in government became the main issue in the coming election, and a full-scale pamphlet war developed. The proposal was approved by the voters in the province as a whole, but Franklin and other supporters of the change were defeated in Philadelphia.

Extensive pamphleteering had been under way ever since the Paxton explosion: Quaker deviltry was "unmasked" by Presbyterian writers, while Quaker partisans were busily furnishing unflattering "looking-glasses" for Presbyterians. Franklin himself had written *A Narrative of the Late Massacres in Lancaster County* . . . (1764), which angered the Scots-Irish, and *Cool Thoughts on the Present Situation of Our Public Affairs* . . . (1764), which alienated all those favorable to the proprietary government and made Franklin a prime target for their polemics. Some of the other important productions of the campaign were: John Dickinson's speech in opposition to the proposed change, which in its printed form had a preface by William Smith, "the Reverend *Sentiment-dresser-General*" of the Proprietary Party; Joseph Galloway's answer to this speech of Dickinson, which was outfitted with a retaliatory preface by Franklin; Dickinson's *Protest against the Appointment of Benjamin Franklin as Agent for the Colony of Pennsylvania* (1764); Franklin's rebuttal to this in his *Remarks on a Late Protest* . . . (1764);

and William Smith's *An Answer to Mr. Franklin's Remarks on a Late Protest.*

The use of personalities by all the combatants generated such violent animosities that Dickinson challenged Galloway to a duel and partisans of both sides were stimulated to produce a rash of outrightly scurrilous pamphlets and broadsides. As the most prominent leader of the anti-Proprietary faction, Franklin got more than his share of attention, and his enemies were accused of trying to blacken his name so that they could succeed more easily in their own nefarious machinations. "In short," said one of Franklin's defenders, "from the tall Knaves of Wealth and Power, to the sneaking Underlings of Corruption, they seem to a Man . . . sworn to load him with all the Filth, and Virulence that the basest Heads and basest Hearts can suggest." The bitterness of the hatred of Franklin is shocking, but it indicates how deeply antipathy toward Franklin was burned into Philadelphia at this early date.

Since he was the champion of basic change in the government, it is not surprising that one of the commonest charges brought against Franklin was that he was "a man so turbulent, and such a plotter, as to be able to embroil the three kingdoms, if he ever has an opportunity." This criticism was stated with considerable restraint and some elegance in the following verses:

> Oh! had he been wise to pursue
> The Track for his Talent designed,
> What a tribute of praise had been due
> To the teacher and friend of mankind.
>
> But to covet political fame
> Was in him a degrading ambition,
> For a spark which from Lucifer came
> Had kindled the blaze of sedition.

A less graceful, but more pointed, bit of doggerel attributes these Machiavellian sentiments to Franklin:

Fight dog, fight bear, you're all my friends;
By you I shall attain my ends;
For I can never be content
Till I have got the government;
But if from this attempt I fall,
Then let the devil take you all!

Numerous changes were rung on this theme, one of which was that Franklin had schemed to have himself appointed governor under a royal charter, with much greater powers than any previous governor had enjoyed. Even Dickinson's formal protest to Franklin's being appointed agent for the colony lamented that "the Peace and Happiness of Pennsylvania should be sacrificed for the Promotion of a Man, who cannot be advanced but by the Convulsions of his Country." And at least one attack on Franklin hinted at the ultimate disaster which might follow from tampering with the governmental structure; it accused him of being a leveler who tried to destroy all distinction and "Every *necessary Subordination....*"

Nor was Franklin's seditiousness an isolated vice; according to his critics it sprang from a thoroughly wicked character. William Smith, for example, accounted for the "odious scurrility" of Franklin's polemics as being the work of "a very bad man, or one delirious with rage, disappointment and malice." Inviting the reader to "make the application where he pleases," Smith concluded his piece by quoting several lines of verse which described a scoundrel of "conscious baseness, conscious vice . . . [within whose breast] All that makes [a] villain found a rest."

Smith also implied that Franklin could be bribed, and all his critics were uneasy about trusting Franklin with public funds. They dwelt at length upon the monetary gains he had already reaped from his official printing and from his missions abroad as agent for the province of Pennsylvania. Some of his enemies seemed to feel that Franklin had taken liberties with his expense account while employed as colonial agent in London from 1757 to 1762. Governor James Hamilton, for example, had at the time ironically observed that Franklin's junketing, his consorting with virtuosi, and his honorary degrees were "no small acquisitions to the public, and therefore well worth paying for."

Hamilton's remarks betray a spiteful jealousy of Franklin's eminent position and his cordial reception by the famous and learned of the Continent. Those who believed themselves possessed of a better title to gentility resented Franklin as an upstart. They spoke slightingly of "his original obscurity," his springing from "the meanest Circumstances," and accounted for his rise by the assistance which better men had so inadvisedly given him, and by Franklin's use of "every Zig Zag Machination" and trimming contrivance of politics.

Most of Franklin's antagonists were likewise unimpressed by his versatility and his scientific achievements. They either alleged that he had begged or purchased his honorary degrees, and had assumed credit for discoveries that was due in justice to other men, or they contented themselves with sarcastic references to "the Philosopher." His electrical experiments furnished the inspiration for many an attempted conceit: Franklin was informed that he should confine himself to "measuring how many quarts of fire were contained in a watery cloud, instead of attempting once more to set this province on fire, that he may have an opportunity of gathering the spoil." John Dickinson was willing to grant Franklin's merit as "a great luminary of the learned world," but he went on to elaborate the metaphor as follows: "Let him still shine, but without wrapping his country in flames. Let him, from a private station, from a smaller sphere, diffuse, as I think he may, a beneficial light; but let him not be made to move and blaze like a comet to terrify and to distress."

But none of the attacks that were made on Franklin's public life and activities could compare in viciousness to those made on his personal morals. It was apparently well known before the battles of 1764 that Franklin had an illegitimate son, and after the campaign began no one could have been ignorant of it. The most odious discussion of Franklin's private life was contained in a scurrilous epitaph on Franklin which was attributed to Hugh Williamson, a teacher of mathematics at the College in Philadelphia and a vigorous champion of the Presbyterian frontiersmen. The writing of such epitaphs became almost a distinct literary genre in Philadelphia during 1764. William Smith seems to have begun it when he composed a laudatory "Epitaph" to the Penn family in his preface to Dickinson's speech opposing the change in government. Franklin replied with his own effort in "the lapidary style," an epitaph contrasting the original Penn with his unworthy descendants; this in turn prompted Williamson to attempt a "small Touch in the Lapidary Way, or Tit for Tat, in your own way," called *What Is Sauce for a Goose Is Also Sauce for a Gander.* This relatively short piece embraced almost all of the categories of Franklin criticism in their most virulent form, and culminated in the suggestion that a household servant named Barbara

was the mother of Franklin's illegitimate son, William. Williamson's juicy morsel then became a source for other contemporary pamphleteers, and for some later historians.

The canon of Franklin criticism in 1764 thus included attacks on his incendiarism, selfish ambition, avarice, scurrility, personal morals, and general wickedness, as well as insulting references to his humble origins and scientific accomplishments. Even more interesting, however, are the omissions from what was later to become the catalogue of his sins. There were in 1764 no attacks on Franklin's religious beliefs, no accusations of deism or atheism. Likewise absent from the contemporary writings was the contempt for Poor Richard's materialistic moralizing which was later to become a staple of Franklin criticism. It is perhaps reasonable to suppose that deism did not become such a heinous offense until the 1790's—the date of Cobbett's attack—when it was allied to Jacobinism; and Poor Richard's bourgeois aspirations probably seemed eminently suitable to Philadelphia in the earlier stages of its growth. But many people were sufficiently outraged at Franklin's politics in 1764 to preserve their animosities and to absorb any other prejudices against him that were developed later.

Besides the Proprietary circle and the Presbyterians, Franklin also made many enemies among the Pennsylvania Germans. This was brought about by a combination of circumstances very unfavorable to the anti-Proprietary faction. Until the period of the French and Indian War, the Germans had been led politically by the Quakers; as more of them moved into the outlying districts, however, they too became subject to Indian incursions, and found their interests coinciding with those of the Scots-Irish.

Their old alliance with the Quakers began to break down, and by 1764 their political allegiance was thoroughly unsettled. At this point the Proprietary forces discovered an earlier writing of Franklin's in which he had made some contemptuous allusions to the Germans; they exploited these remarks with an effectiveness that stunned their author. In reporting his defeat at the polls to Richard Jackson, Franklin exclaimed: "They carried (would you think it!) above 1000 Dutch from me. . . ."

In the passage which caused all the trouble, Franklin had asked, "why should the *Palatine Boors* be suffered to swarm into our Settlements and, by herding together, establish their Language and Manners, to the Exclusion of ours?" The Proprietary forces circulated these remarks with great industry; according to one writer they "attend[ed] every night at the *Dutch* Coffee-House, to inculcate that Paper with their own observations on it." "Their own observations" took the form of helpful translations which rendered "boors" in the most unfavorable light possible. Franklin alleged that his enemies had told the Germans that he had called them "a *Herd of Hogs*," and a versifier friendly to Franklin made the same charge in a piece called *The Plot*. This work portrayed two Proprietary minions who conceived a scheme to defeat Franklin by blasting his credit with the Germans. "Here," said one of them, pointing to a magazine, "he has call'd them *Boors*, that's *Hogs*." The other thought the idea splendid, and the two of them began to collar the Germans and read them the exceptionable passage. The plot failed, though, according to the writer, who sketched the scene thus:

> At what we read they only stare,
> Not one with F. . . . .n seems offended,
> At length *Hans* who knew *English* better,

Clear'd the Point with his V̄isage pleasant,
Your *Wisdoms* have mistook a Letter [,]
Boar may be Hogs but *Boor* is Peasant.
Thus was the deep laid PLOT Confounded,
A PLOT that promis'd once so well,
With a dutch Laugh the Street resounded.

But the Germans were not so easily pacified as the writer of *The Plot* pretended; they were being wooed vigorously by the Proprietary faction, who immediately supplied *An Answer to the Plot*. The *Answer*, which ignored the linguistic problem completely, began reasonably enough by observing that:

> Whilst busy Cits neglect their Shop,
>   To turn State Politicians,
> No human Arts on Earth can Stop
>   The Growth of our Divisions.

This equable tone was soon abandoned, however, in favor of a noisome attack upon Franklin's moral life. Franklin was described as "a Letcher" who "Needs nothing to excite him, / But is too ready to engage, / When younger Arms envite him"; the Germans were therefore advised to use "All Female soft Perswasion, / To draw F . . . . . . n from raising News, / To mind his Occupation."

The translation of "boors" was dealt with more adequately in numerous German-language pamphlets. The chief point at issue here was whether it was true, as the pro-Franklin writers argued, that "the English word 'boors' means nothing more than 'peasants' *(Bauren [sic])*." Franklin's German friends not only softened the force of the expression he had used, they palliated his strictures against the Germans by avowing that the more recent immigrants were a less desirable class than the earlier group, and that many of Pennsylvania's Germans were themselves displeased with the newer arrivals. It was also pointed out that Franklin had treated the Germans well before and had gotten them good wages for their supply service in the Braddock campaign. The Proprietary forces were really the ones who held the Germans in contempt, these writers declared, and they had abused the Germans in print much more harshly than Franklin had.

German writers opposed to Franklin presented a different version; they asserted that he had done the Germans many injuries and blamed him for all their woes. He was said to be responsible for the underrepresentation of the back country, because many Germans lived there, and Franklin could not bear "that our fellow countrymen should sit in the Assembly." Even the high cost of postage to the fatherland was attributed to Franklin. The other factors involved in the change of government were not, of course, overlooked by German pamphleteers, but Franklin's role became the focal point of the discussion. One writer reviewed Franklin's offenses and concluded, with heavy sarcasm, that the Germans would no doubt wish to "swarm" into the city on election day and "herd together" at the polls to elect their good friend Franklin. The Germans did vote in large numbers, but they voted against Franklin; since the margin of his defeat was slim, their influence was probably decisive. Nor was the matter soon forgotten; Franklin's "boorish" remarks still embarrassed his supporters a year later, when they found it necessary to explain: "'Tis well known that *Boor* means no more than a Country Farmer; and that *herding* signifies flocking or gathering together, and is applied by the best English Writers to harmless Doves, or Ladies in Distress."

Franklin, of course, had many defenders in 1764; but it is likely that the principal effect of their polemical efforts was to make his enemies more bitter rather than to win him any new friends. For these were none of the "prim" people from whom Carl Van Doren was concerned to rescue Franklin; they resorted to the same sort of savage *"Bush Fighting,"* as one of them called it, that was used by the Proprietary champions. They made the author of the slanderous assault on Franklin, *What Is Sauce for a Goose,* the subject of an equally vicious epitaph; and the same person was elsewhere characterized as "a Reptile," who had tried "like a Toad, by the pestilential Fumes of his virulent Slabber, [to] blast the Fame of a PATRIOT."

Isaac Hunt, father of the poet Leigh Hunt, became the chief defender of Franklin's reputation, but his methods were such that he probably did more to exacerbate the anti-Franklin feeling than to dissipate it. Hunt was quite extreme in his attacks on the Presbyterians and on Franklin's enemies in the influential governor's circle. Upper-class distaste for Franklin was no doubt intensified when Hunt devoted thirteen verses of scurrilous billingsgate to William Allen, who stood at the forefront of Philadelphia aristocracy. Hunt called Allen, who was chief justice of Pennsylvania, the "GRAND CALUMNIATOR-GENERAL" of the province, and portrayed him as dishonest, immoral, and a stutterer. The attack on the aristocracy became more inclusive when Hunt furnished a genealogical register of some of Philadelphia's leading families, identifying in their backgrounds London fishwives, huckstering salt sellers, and daughters of convict servants.

The savage attacks on Franklin had put his friends on the defensive, and if they did not wish to descend to the level of Hunt, there was little they could do but deny the opposition's calumnies and assert that Franklin was a good man and a great patriot who could "look down on such his Enemies with conscious Superiority, and laugh at them. . . ." But Franklin and his supporters had one dramatic moment of glory which was raised into a sort of symbolic triumph. Although he was defeated in the election, Franklin was reappointed immediately afterward as provincial agent to England. He departed on November 7, 1764, and three hundred well-wishers accompanied him to Chester where he took ship, giving him a rousing demonstration of their loyalty and esteem. A letter written by one of the participants in this triumph gives a stirring description of the scene. Franklin, according to this anonymous witness, "was attended by a very great Number of the reputable Inhabitants of this City and County; and on his embarking, was saluted by a Number of Cannon, and the Huzza's of the People; and an Anthem was sung, (composed here) suitable to the Occasion. He was rowed on board the Ship *King of Prussia* . . . . by Ten Freeholders of the White-Oak Company, in their Barge, they attending on Purpose; in short, the Respect that was paid to this great and truly deserving Patriot, can hardly be set forth, nor the Joys shewn on the Occasion, be express'd."

The writer then explained that Franklin was to carry to London the petition for changing the government of Pennsylvania, and he added that Franklin might also "by his great Influence and Abilities," obtain some relief from the recent acts of Parliament, the Grenville acts. But, in any event, it was reassuring to know "that a Man is gone Home, who will neither spare Labour nor Pains," in working for his countrymen. Even the opposition in Pennsylvania had become "very quiet, and left off abusing . . . the Character of one of the best and greatest Men of *America*. . . ."

The text of "The Anthem Sung at Chester," the best literary expression of honor and respect for Franklin produced in the 1764 campaign, is also provided by this witness:

O LORD our GOD arise,
Scatter our Enemies,
    And make them fall.
Confound their Politicks,
Frustrate such Hypocrites,
Franklin, on Thee we fix,
    GOD Save us all.

Thy Knowledge rich in Store,
On *Pennsylvania* pour,
    Thou [*sic*] great Blessing:
Long to defend our Laws,
Still give us greater Cause,
To sing with Heart and Voice,
    GEORGE and *FRANKLIN*

GOD Save Great *GEORGE* our King;
Prosper agent FRANKLIN;
    Grant him Success:
Hark how the Vallies ring;
GOD Save our Gracious King,
From whom all Blessings spring,
    Our Wrongs redress.

The ship, her sails filled with good wishes, made a rapid passage, and in London, Franklin stepped into a larger theater than provincial Pennsylvania. He was not to return until years later, when he had won a world-wide reputation by his statesmanship. Although the animosities that had been so deeply burned into the hearts of Philadelphians were long remembered, and "hereditary prejudices" survived "by a mysterious kind of atavism," perhaps even into our own day, still Franklin's stature has not been permanently effaced by his enemies' virulence. One of Franklin's old friends declared after the election, "thy Integer Vita will be thy preservation, and Eclipse . . . [thy opponents'] Tinsell'd Glory." The passage of almost two centuries has justified the confidence of Franklin's friend.

WILLIAM CARLOS WILLIAMS (1883–1963), American poet and writer who was also a physician, sets forth a critical view of Franklin as a pioneer statesman. Franklin's influential writings stressing thrift and practicality have encouraged Americans to busy themselves in building walls to keep out "the terrible beauty of the New World." Almost nothing is left of the great wilderness except the memory of the American Indian. Is Williams justified in claiming that fear was the driving force in Franklin's personality? Can the present ecological dilemma faced by Americans be identified with the Franklin spirit of extreme practicality that encouraged exploitation of our virgin lands?*

William Carlos Williams

Franklin and Rejection of the American Wilderness

"He's sort of proud of his commonness, isn't he?"

He was the balancer full of motion without direction, the gyroscope which by its large spinning kept us, at that early period of our fate, upon an even keel.

The greatest winner of his day, he represents a voluptuousness of omnivorous energy brought to a dead stop by the rock of New World inopportunity. His energy never attained to a penetrant gist; rather it was stopped by and splashed upon the barrier, like a melon. His "good" was scattered about him. This is what is called being "practical." At such "success" we smile to see Franklin often so puffed up.

In the sheer mass of his voluptuous energy lies his chief excuse—a trait he borrowed without recognition from the primitive profusion of his surroundings.

Relaxed in a mass of impedimenta he found opportunity for thought.

Franklin, along with all the responsible aristocrats of his period, shows the two major characteristics of a bulky, crude energy, something in proportion to the continent, and a colossal restraint equalizing it. The result must have been a complete cancellation, frustration or descent to a low plane for release, which latter alternative he chose shiningly.

He played with lightning and the French court.

The great force (which was in him the expression of the New World) must have had not only volume but a quality, the determination of which will identify him. It was in Franklin, as shown characteristically in this letter, a scattering to reconnoitre.

Poor Richard's Almanac was as important in founding the nation as Paine's *Age of Reason*—he adaged them into a kind of pride in possession.

By casting scorn at men merely of birth while stressing the foundation of estates which should be family strongholds he did the service of discouraging aristocracy and creating it—the qualifying condition being that he repelled that which was foreign and supported that which was native—on a lower level FOR THE TIME BEING. He sparred for time: he was a diplomat of distinction with positive New World characteristics.

His mind was ALL out of the New World. Feeling a strength, a backing which was the New itself, he could afford to be sly with France, England or any nation; since, to live, he had to be sly with the massive strength of that primitive wilderness with whose conditions he had been bred to battle: thus, used to a mass EQUAL to them, he could swing them too. So again he asserted his nativity.

Strong and New World in innate strength, he is without beauty. The force of the New World is never in these men open; it is sly, covert, almost cringing. It is the mass that forces them into praise of mediocrity to escape its compulsions: so there is a kind of nastiness in his TOUCHING the hand of the Marchioness, in his meddling with the lightning, a resentment against his upstart bumptiousness in advising London how to light its stupidly ill-lit streets.

There has not yet appeared in the New World any one with sufficient strength for the open assertion. So with Franklin, the tone is frightened and horribly smug—at his worst; it flames a little in de Soto; it is necessary to Boone to lose himself in the wilds; there are no women —Houston's bride is frightened off; the New Englanders are the clever bone-men. Nowhere the open, free assertion save in the Indian: this is the quality. Jones has to leave the American navy, we feel, to go to Russia, for release.

It is necessary in appraising our history to realize that the nation was the offspring of the desire to huddle, to protect—of terror—superadded to a new world of great beauty and ripest blossom that well-nigh no man of distinction saw save Boone.

Franklin is the full development of the timidity, the strength that denies itself.

Such is his itch to serve science.

"Education" represented to these pioneers an *obscure* knowledge of the great beauty that was denied them, but of the great beauty under their feet no man seems to have been conscious, to appreciable degree; the foundation they must *first* appraise.

Nowhere does the full assertion come through save as a joke, jokingly, that masks the rest.

The terrible beauty of the New World attracts men to their ruin. Franklin did not care to be ruined—he only wanted to touch.

"I wish he hadn't gone fooling with lightning; I wish he'd left it alone—the old fool." Sure enough, he didn't dare let it go in at the top of his head and out at his toes, that's it; he *had* to fool with it. He sensed the power and knew only enough to want to run an engine with it. His fingers itched to be meddling, to do the little concrete thing—the barrier against a flood of lightning that would innundate him. Of course he was the most useful, "the most industrious citizen that Philadelphia or America had ever known." He was the dike keeper, keeping out the wilderness with his wits. Fear drove his curiosity.

Do something, anything, to keep the fingers busy—not to realize—the lightning. Be industrious, let money and comfort increase; money is like a bell that keeps the dance from terrifying, as it would if it were silent and we could hear the grunt—thud—swish. It is small, hard; it keeps the attention fixed so that the eyes shall not see. And such is humor: pennies—that see gold come of copper by adding together, shrewd guesses hidden under the armament of a humble jest.

Poor Richard.

Don't offend.

His mighty answer to the New World's offer of a great embrace was THRIFT. Work night and day, build up, penny by penny, a wall against that which is threatening, the terror of life, poverty. Make a fort to be secure in

The terrific energy of the new breed is its first character; the second is its terror before the NEW.

As a boy, he had tentatively loosed himself once to love, to curiosity perhaps, which was the birth of his first son. But the terror of that dare must have frightened the soul out of him. Having dared that once, his heart recoiled; his teaching must have smitten him. But Franklin, shrewd fellow, did not succumb to the benumbing judgment and go branded, repentant or rebellious. He trotted off gaily to Philly and noticed Bettsy in the shop on Arch Street, the first day.

He is our wise prophet of chicanery, the great buffoon, the face on the penny stamp.

The shock his youth got went into the fibre of the Constitution: he joked himself into a rich life—so he joked the country into a good alliance: to fortify, to buckle up—and reserve a will to be gay, to BE—(on the side).

Poor Richard: Save, be rich—and do as you please—might have been his motto, with an addendum: provided your house has strong walls and thick shutters.

Prince Richard in the lamb's skin: with a tongue in the cheek for aristocracy, humbly, arrogantly (that you may wish to imitate me) touching everything.

To want to touch, not to wish anything to remain clean, aloof—comes always of a kind of timidity, from fear.

The character they had (our pioneer statesmen, etc.) was that of giving their fine energy, as they must have done, to the smaller, narrower, protective thing and not to the great, New World. Yet they cannot quite leave hands off it but must TOUCH it, in a "practical" way, that is a joking, shy, nasty way, using "science" etc., not with the generosity of the savage or scientist but in a shameful manner. The sweep of the force was too horrible to them; it would have swept them into chaos. They HAD to do as they *could* but it can be no offense that their quality should be *named*. They could have been inspired by the new QUALITY about them to yield to loveliness in a fresh spirit.

It is the placing of his enthusiasm that characterizes the man.

It is not to mark Franklin, but to attempt to appraise the nature of the difficulties that molded him, the characteristic *weight of the mass;* how nearly all our national heroes have been driven back—and praised by reason of their shrewdness in making walls: not in bursting into flower.

To discover the NEW WORLD: that there is something there: what it has done to us, its quality, its weight, its prophets, its—horrible temper.

The niggardliness of our history, our

stupidity, sluggishness of spirit, the false-ness of our historical notes, the complete missing of the point. Addressed to the wrong head, the tenacity with which the fear still inspires laws, customs—the suppression of the superb corn dance of the Chippewas, since it symbolizes the generative processes—as if morals have but one character, and that—SEX: while morals are deformed in the name of PURITY; till, in the confusion, almost nothing remains of the great American New World but a memory of the Indian.

F. L. LUCAS (1894–1967), distinguished English scholar
and writer, is a friendly critic who sees Franklin as a
many-sided man who had two loves, science and
America. Despite Franklin's relative indifference to art,
literature, and the beauties of nature, he achieved a
happy balance in life by combining practicality with
speculative thought. Why does Lucas feel that the world
could use many more Franklins?*

F. L. Lucas

Franklin: A Man of Good Sense

"I, Benjamin Franklin, of Philadelphia,
printer, late Minister Plenipotentiary
from the United States of America to the
Court of France, now President of the
State of Pennsylvania"—so begins the will
drawn up by the old statesman in July
1788, two years before he died.

"Printer . . . Plenipotentiary . . . President"—the wording is typical. Franklin
had too much good sense to conceal the
inky fingers with which his long career
had begun. And he was too human not to
feel a just pride in that long ascent from
printer to President; too genuine to disguise the just pride that he felt. He had,
indeed, left his lasting imprint on the
Western Hemisphere. Yet, unlike most
great men, and many successful men, he
had also succeeded in being happy. Johnson would not have repeated a single week
of his own life, not though an angel offered; but Franklin would, he said, have
been willing to run through his again—
wishing, if possible, to have an author's
privilege of emending certain *errata;* yet
ready for a repetition, even were that
denied.

Perhaps he lacked imagination; perhaps he would have refused, after all, had
it really been possible to live over again.
Yet he must have thought what he said;
for Franklin was honest. And to have got
so much zest from a life of over eighty
years is perhaps still more remarkable
than for a tallow-chandler's son to have
disarmed the lightning, and checkmated
a king.

Here, indeed, is a typical sage of the

*From F. L. Lucas, *The Art of Living: Four Eighteenth-Century Minds* (New York: The Macmillan
Company, 1960), pp. 205–207, 255–260. Footnotes omitted.

89

Century of Sense and Prose—yet free from its endemic melancholy, its hypochondria, its spleen. Franklin was not quite as unpoetic as the young Bentham, who watched him on that dramatic day in 1774 when the quiet American was baited in the Cockpit by Wedderburn before ministers and Privy Councillors. Franklin could enjoy the verse of Thomson and Cowper; he could turn out verses of a kind himself; yet his mind remained essentially prosaic, and his strength is the strength of firm-based prose.

Indeed, contemplating his life, one may suspect, like Jane Austen, that *too* deep an absorption in poetry does not often bring much happiness—pleasure, no doubt; at times, even joy; but, perhaps, not much lasting happiness. Poetry can console, enchant, ennoble; it can transfigure the world with the magic of moonlight; but its greatest lovers are seldom the most cheerful or most practical of men—as Franklin *was*.

Nor, though it was his early ambition to become a prose stylist, did Franklin greatly care about even prose literature, or art, for their own sakes. "And, for one," he writes, "I confess, that if I could find in any Italian travels a receipt for making Parmesan cheese, it would give me more satisfaction than a transcript of any inscription from any old stone whatever." Flaubert might have thought this a perfect gem of bourgeois fatuity.

But at least Franklin was as plainspoken and downright as his name. And since the world has far more art than any lifetime can cope with, but infinitely less honesty and intelligence than it urgently needs, I am not on that account disposed to disparage him.

Nor did Franklin feel much, apparently, for the loveliness of Nature. It is characteristic that he employed Wordsworth's Derwentwater, not as a theme for poetic feeling, but as a surface to cast oil on, in an experiment for calming troubled waters.

Yet one should not exaggerate Franklin's lack of the imaginative. The kind of imagination that shows itself in whimsical humour, in graceful wit, in vivid apologue and illustration, was his to a high degree. Only he remained essentially an efficient, extroverted person, who preferred to any other art the art—some might say, the craft—of living; perpetually curious of new truths, fundamentally impatient of the vague, the rapturous, the futile. Johnson, no doubt, thought him a Whig dog of the most vicious kind; but Franklin, though far calmer, saner, more practical, remains far nearer to Johnson than to ethereal souls like Shelley. Which type one prefers is a matter of private feeling and judgement; one may be glad that mankind, in its infinite variety, can produce both.

Franklin's two great loves were Science and America. Both are present in Turgot's famous line on him—

Eripuit caelo fulmen, sceptrumque tyrannis.
(He snatched from Heaven the lightning, the sceptre from tyrants' hands.)

Franklin's modesty at once disclaimed this hyperbolic praise—the lightning, he said, still fell; and he was only one among thousands who helped to break the power of George III. Still that epigram keeps more truth than many. To-day, indeed, Franklin might be less wholly happy about those two great causes. Science, since then, has grown too strong, and too mixed a blessing; and the United States have perhaps grown too big—not, indeed, for the defence of Western freedom, but for their own well-being. Yet, on balance, he might still be content.

But Franklin himself remains of more than historic interest. For he is also a standing example of a man of good will, who laboured fruitfully for the lives of his fellows, and for his own as well. Saints have often been slightly foolish or perverse; one may prefer sages. And Franklin was a sage. He found happiness, as it is best found, by health of mind and body, by activity in the service of others, by a versatility which preserved him from our modern disease of specialist's cramp. Printing, commerce, public service, diplomacy, mathematics, electricity, meteorology, astronomy, geology, ethnology, education, physics, chemistry, agriculture, medicine, hygiene, navigation, aeronautics, cookery—even this does not exhaust the long list of his activities. He recalls the happy versatility of the Renaissance. To-day his work is long since done, his discoveries obsolete; yet from the life of Benjamin Franklin there is still, I think, much to be learned. . . .

Why was it . . . that Franklin would have been willing . . . to live his life again, and Johnson not?

Johnson's career, like those of Boswell or Gray, leaves, I think, with all our admiration for their qualities, a certain sense of frustration that those qualities yet failed, so completely, to bring satisfaction or content. Whereas the careers of Franklin, Gibbon, or Hume, possess, on the contrary, a satisfying balance, an artistic completeness, that seem characteristically eighteenth-century.

One may say, of course, that the contrast was largely luck. But "luck" means merely the unlikely convergence of certain trains of causation. And when, over a long period, men are consistently fortunate or the reverse, it generally means that they have an inward tendency to play well, or ill, the cards that life deals to them.

The differences in these six lives turn mainly on the presence or absence of health, mental and bodily; of good sense; of affection; and of effectiveness in serving others, as well as themselves.

In bodily health, Johnson and Gray were unlucky from birth. Boswell wrecked his. But Hume, Gibbon, and Franklin were more fortunate; though even they might have given the matter more thought (as Franklin confessed in his dialogue with the Gout). They loved the table too well. But it is a mistake to grow fat.

Mentally, Johnson, Gray, and Boswell all suffered from a neurotic melancholia, which made them often unhappy in this world, and made two of them unhappy about the next; in contrast to the natural gaiety of the other three. Happiness, indeed, depends more on temperament than on reason. Yet lack of practical good sense can produce circumstances where happiness becomes difficult, even for temperaments as gay as Goldsmith's.

Hume and Gibbon both played their cards prudently; but here perhaps Franklin stands out, as the very incarnation of prudence.

No doubt, he too could be led by violent feeling into follies. He too could commit his "errata"; and pay too much, at times, for his "whistles." Yet without that warmth of feeling his prudence might have become repellent to others, boring to himself. On the other hand, he had none of that false shame about good sense as something somehow mean, ridiculous, or prosaic, which has made many men prefer to be foolish. Typical is the method of reaching a decision in difficult dilemmas which he propounded in a letter to Priestley—his "moral or prudential algebra." This consisted in taking a sheet of paper; dividing it into two columns, "Pro" and "Con"; filling one with the reasons for doing the thing in question and the other with the reasons against; and then cancelling those that seemed equal or, say, two reasons on one side against three slightly less weighty on the other; the advantage being that in this way one can consider two or more factors simultaneously, whereas the ordinary person thinks only of one at a time, and veers endlessly back and forth. I own that I have never tried this, any more than Franklin's scheme for reaching moral perfection. Perhaps one is too shy of being too methodical and mechanical. At all events, when one contrasts Franklin's ways with the catalogues of human imbecilities that make up half of every morning's newspaper, I find myself in warm sympathy with his cry of exasperation, provoked by the pig-headedness of certain Dover postilions—

They added other Reasons, that were no Reasons at all, and made me, as upon a hundred other Occasions, almost wish that Mankind had never been endow'd with a reasoning Faculty, since they know so little how to make use of it, and so often mislead themselves by it, and that they had been furnish'd with a good sensible Instinct instead of it.

In personal relations, Johnson was warm-hearted, but too dictatorial; Boswell, mercurial and philandering, became sadly conscious that in a self-defeating way he cheapened himself, and seldom won fondness without an admixture of contempt; Gray was caged in his own shyness. In contrast, "le bon David" charmed even his enemies; Gibbon might fail Suzanne Curchod, but his physical grotesqueness did not impair the warm ties that bound him to his stepmother, to Deyverdun, to Lord Sheffield; and Franklin with his shrewd simplicity and his whimsical fondness won hearts not only in his own countries of America and England, but even in critical and aristocratic France.

Still, for happiness, love alone is, in the long run, seldom sufficient; there is need also for activity, preferably activity of some use in the world. For men are also gregarious, social creatures. Johnson, however, though he toiled heroically, was haunted by a guilty sense of idleness and waste. Boswell, though he kept his journals, frittered away his days. And Gray was thwarted by the niggardliness of his poetic inspiration; while the learning he piled on learning, like a miser's riches, was a means of killing his time rather than of enriching his life. He could acquire knowledge; but he could not impart it, living, nor keep it, dead. Gibbon, by contrast, did his job (though he did not like it much) as captain of Hampshire grenadiers; and was rewarded by being the better able to do his real job of reviving a dead Rome, and writing a history which survives all that modern research can find to correct in it. Hume, having done for philosophy the best service perhaps that can be done for it, by proving the futility of much of it, was not only an effective public servant, but also played a lasting part in diffusing tolerance and sense. And Franklin, as scientist, diplomat, patriot, and humanitarian, was probably the happiest of them all, in seeing, before he died, the new world he had largely created, and finding it good. Perhaps, even his balanced judgement was slightly carried away by the optimism of the time. "Thank God," he wrote to his French friend, Le Veillard, in 1788, "the world is growing wiser and wiser: and as by degrees men are convinced of the folly of wars for religion, for domination, or for commerce, they will be happier and happier." Le Veillard was to be guillotined.

But if Franklin became over-optimistic, this was for him a pleasant error. Possibly his hopes merely ante-dated a saner future: possibly they were only a kindly dream. But at least they lasted his time.

It may, of course, be felt that Franklin, despite his occasional rhyming, suffered from a certain lack of poetry. Yet, he enjoyed Thomson.

"Whatever Thomson writes," says a letter to Strahan in 1744, "send me a dozen copies of. I had read no poetry for several years, and almost lost the Relish of it, till I met with his *Seasons*. That charming Poet has brought more Tears of Pleasure into my Eyes than all I ever read before. I wish it were in my Power to return him any Part of the joy he has given me."

And again as an old man in 1782, when "the relish for reading poetry had long left me," he enjoyed Cowper's *Poems,* and read them all, some more than once. He had also strong, if simple, tastes in music; he himself played guitar, harp, and violin. His improvements in the harmonica (musical glasses) may have been partly love of mechanics as well as of art. All the same there remains no tale of him more typical than that which tells how the town of Franklin, having taken his name, asked him to send them church-bells—and received instead a consignment of books; on the ground that "sense is better than sound." Some may have disapproved that sober jest; some will disapprove it still. But I shall not join them.

Franklin may be regarded, like Hume, as on the whole a prosaic person. And so to-day he is far less of an influence in the world than, say, Wordsworth. It is of the nature of scientific or political successes that time leaves them behind, superseded. On the other hand, it is easy to exaggerate this aspect. The literary forget how much poetry, also, dies of old age; and how tiny a fragment even of civilized populations cares a pin for poetry. Indeed, there may well be far more to-day who believe in astrology.

Again, there is more good poetry in existence than the world has time for. The supply has long exceeded the demand. For though time slowly gnaws even at poetry, it is a durable thing—like York Minster—which centuries do not make obsolete. Further, however much we owe, and go on owing, to a poet like Wordsworth, it is common enough for poets not to be in other ways the most admirable or attractive of men. I would far rather have the life of a Franklin than of a Wordsworth; I would far rather live with a Franklin than with a Wordsworth. I suspect, indeed, that Wordsworth, like many of his fellow-bards, would have been most trying to live with.

Nor, even if Franklin seems prosaic, was his life without imagination. He had those imaginative gifts without which it is impossible to become either a scientific discoverer, or a far-sighted statesman; and his playful fancy was probably more effective at redeeming life, for him and his, from dulness, than even the poetic imagination of most poets.

And so there is not only fascination in following his passage through life, there is also a good deal to admire—his many-sidedness; his balance; his happy combination of speculative thought and practical action, which saved him from the irritable frustration common among men too exclusively theoretical or imaginative. "I will disinherit you," said Sydney Smith to his daughter, "if you do not admire everything written by Franklin." Sydney Smith was given to humorous exaggeration; but he was a man of sense.

It seems to me that our world might gain a good deal in well-being from a multiplication of Franklins. That is why I thought it not unreasonable to redress the balance of this series of literary portraits by calling in from the New World a figure far less literary, yet in some ways still more alive—the Socrates, the Timoleon, and the Archimedes of America.

A very different view, as might be expected, was taken by D. H. Lawrence. Like Carlyle, he saw in Franklin "the father of all the Yankees;" but, more vehement even than Carlyle, he saw the United States as a nation of dreary, futile, muck-raking dummies, hustling and bustling, ape-like, about a colossal cage. "The pattern American," writes Lawrence, "this dry, moral, utilitarian little democrat, has done more to ruin the old Europe than any Russian nihilist." He is particularly outraged by Franklin's homely list of virtues; which he replaces by thirteen improved rules of his own—for example, "Cleanliness. Don't be too clean. It impoverishes the blood." This, if not science, is at least candour.

The gulf, of course, between types so opposite as Franklin and Lawrence remains unbridgeable. There can hardly be reconciliation between those who value, above all, "fire in the belly" and those who value light in the brain. Lawrence liked to picture himself as a wolf with red eyes, and as a dark forest full of multitudes of selves and strange gods, including the Holy Ghost; whereas Franklin, he thought, subconsciously hated Europe and set out to destroy it. Hence Lawrence's conclusion—"Let Hell loose and get your own back, Europe!" To this kindly wish I suppose Franklin might have replied with a smile that, like King George in 1775, Europe did "let Hell loose" in 1914 and 1939—and only strengthened America. What Europe "got back" is less apparent. As for "subconsciously hating" that Europe in which he lived a quarter of a century, and several times considered settling for life, even were this pretty theory true, Franklin might have asked why it should be wicked for him to hate Europe, yet right for Lawrence to hate so much of America.

But the debate is idle. I suppose one should be grateful for the infinite variety of human nature—though I own I should not much lament a world without Lawrences. Too many Franklins—too many of any type—would grow monotonous. But the risk of many Franklins seems remote. I think we could do with a good many more.

ESMOND WRIGHT (b. 1915), member of Parliament
and professor of modern history at the University of
Glasgow, shows that Franklin's preoccupation with
self-discipline, personal success, and reputation, was
typical of the eighteenth century though we tend to
find it distasteful today. Franklin's great versatility is
also suspect in our own age of specialization. Wright
thus sees Franklin as an eighteenth-century figure.
However, he contends that in some respects Franklin
is particularly modern. On what grounds does he
justify Franklin's modernity?*

Esmond Wright

Franklin: The Self-made Man

Benjamin Franklin, to his contemporaries the greatest figure America had yet produced, was born two hundred and fifty years ago, in January 1706. Publisher, printer, essayist and author, scientist, philologist, politician, "General," diplomat, Fellow of the Royal Society, Doctor of Laws of Oxford and St. Andrews, federalist, though not in a party sense, in all the rôles he played he remained still very much himself. In his range, his origins, his success, Franklin seemed to be the living answer to Hector St. John de Crevecoeur's famous question in 1784, "What then *is* the American, this new man? David Hume thought Franklin "the first philosopher, and indeed the first great man of letters for whom we are beholden to America." Some of his own compatriots bracketed him with Washington, but honest, splenetic John Adams wrote, rather spitefully, to Dr. Rush, "The history of our Revolution will be one continued lie from one end to the other. The essence of the whole will be that Dr. Franklin's electrical rod smote the earth and out sprang General Washington. That Franklin electrified him with his rod, and thenceforward these two conducted all the policy, negotiations, legislatures, and war." He admitted Franklin's genius, original, sagacious, inventive, but he could not see where his excellence lay as legislator or as politician or as negotiator. "From day to day he sat in silence at the Continental Congress,"

*From Esmond Wright, "Benjamin Franklin: A Tradesman in the Age of Reason," in *History Today*, Peter Quennell and Abn Hodge, eds., Vol. VI, No. 7 (July, 1956), pp. 439–447.

he said, "a great part of his time fast asleep in his chair," and in France he was too self-indulgent to attend regularly to the business of the embassy.

Later biographers have described him in more kindly terms and in a variety of ways—*Franklin, the Apostle of Modern Times,* Father of American Democracy, The Many-Sided Franklin, Socrates at the Printing Press, Father of American Ingenuity, The first high priest of the religion of efficiency, or even *Franklin, the First Civilized American.* For Franklin's success was striking. Born with no advantages, he helped to unite his newly independent country, and to conclude an alliance with France which greatly contributed to American victory in 1783; he became a lion in the literary world of Paris; and he acted as conciliator at large and Founding Father Extraordinary in the debates over the Constitution at Philadelphia in 1787. Yet, despite services almost as great as Washington's, references to him in academic circles in the United States were greeted, until recently at least, with a denigrating smile and a raised eyebrow. Where then does Franklin's reputation stand one quarter of a millennium after his birth?

Franklin's very versatility is suspect in our own more specialist age. In the eighteenth century it was still possible for a man to take all learning to be his province; easier in America than in Europe, and easier there to earn the reputation, like Jefferson, of being a man of parts. Today this catholic range is discredited; Franklin's scientific experiments, his identification of electricity and lightning, his study of solar heat, of ocean currents, of the causes of storms, his interest in population studies and statistics are dismissed as the amateur dabblings of a superficial scientist.

There is more abundant cause for the raising of eyebrows. Franklin was born, unsuitably as it proved, in Puritan Boston, the tenth son and seventeenth child of a tallow chandler and soap boiler who had emigrated from Northampton, and baptized in Boston's Old South Church. Despite this favourable beginning, his youthful character was not all that it might have been. He was apprenticed to an elder brother, a printer, but relations were never harmonious; he became as egotistical as he was precocious —as an old man looking back on the past he told his son, "I do not remember when I could not read." He ran away to distant Philadelphia; he embezzled money; he had an illegitimate son William, born in the same year as the father was attempting a literary work called *The Art of Virtue,* a son of whom he was very fond, but who later became, through Bute's influence, Governor of New Jersey and a royalist, and later still, himself the father of an illegitimate son. Franklin never lost his interest in women; Cobbett, at the time a bitter Federalist pamphleteer in Philadelphia, could refer to him seven years after his death as "a crafty and lecherous old hypocrite . . . whose very statue seems to gloat on the wenches as they walk the State House yard." If never vain, he was certainly not untouched by flattery, in Philadelphia or France. He remained a racy and roguish figure to the end, and rarely chose to hide his indiscretions. It is not a picture to everyone's taste, and the distaste is increased by Franklin's sententiousness, his proneness to give advice—much sought, especially when, over seventy, he was the most popular man in Paris. La Rochefoucauld's maxim of a century before— "Old men are fond of giving good advice, because they are no longer in a position to set bad examples"—applies all too aptly.

Perhaps what is at the root of this distaste is the difficulty our own century finds in understanding the pre-occupation of the eighteenth century with personal success and reputation, and in understanding the eighteenth-century American view of character and behaviour. In our own day, living in crowded cities and faced with the menace of routine and mechanical processes, we have put an emphasis on spontaneity, on a man's native gifts for life, on untrammelled self-expression. Eighteenth-century Americans would have regarded this as naïve, for they had no illusions about the need for discipline, or about the motives that drove men to seek success and influence. Indeed what the colonial frontier taught was that either you learn to discipline yourself or you die. To lose patience with the elements in a rough sea off Cape Cod, or with Indians on the forest trails of the Alleghenies, was to lose your life. America bred political freedom, but in practical matters it bred caution and patience, judgment and discretion, tolerance and *finesse*, and it was on these qualities that successful careers were built. Americans then strove as much for self-restraint and self-mastery as for self-government. Witness the career of Washington on the one hand, and his concern with what he called his "honour"; witness the observations of Paine and Jefferson on the other. However divided on matters of political interpretation they might be, all would have shared a common respect for the qualities of discipline and balance; all recognized in their own natures how their instincts had to be curbed by reason. Reputations were made the hard way by deliberate character-training. Witness again Washington's laborious Rules of Civility, the hundred or more rules by which social success might be achieved. There are obvious parallels here with Boswell and Rousseau and Lord Chesterfield.

When Benjamin Franklin devised *Poor Richard* and used him as a vehicle of exhortation and advice—and when from time to time he revealed how hard self-control was for himself—his fellows knew what he meant. He was a practical man, writing in his annual periodical *Poor Richard's Almanac,* for other practical men. Frankly-recognized natural instincts should, indeed must, be harnessed, if a reputation was to be made and merited. And this, the self-reliance that originated as a frontier gospel, became the key doctrine of American Transcendentalism. Franklin's disciple is Emerson, as Carlyle saw; if Emerson rejected Franklin's man because "he savoured of nothing heroic," *Poor Richard* still lives on, with sanctity added to sanctimoniousness, in the pages of *The Journals.* In the *Almanac* Franklin printed common-sense observations and wise saws, culled mainly from Rabelais and Swift and Sterne—and he did not pretend to originality. He made it, in fact, the first great syndicated column in American journalism. He wrote with unerring skill and great charm for the colonial equivalent of the man in the street, in this case the man on the farm and on the frontier. He wrote easily on half a hundred topics—*Dissertation on Liberty and Necessity, Pleasure and Pain, the Way to Wealth, On the Causes and Cure of Smoky Chimneys.* He became a folk-philosopher, sharper than Confucius, more ruminative than Dale Carnegie. The middle-class morality, which Shaw and D. H. Lawrence pilloried but which is still at the vital roots of American prosperity, and which is reflected in its industry, its native shrewdness, its frugality, its practicality, can be said to find its first prophet in Benjamin Franklin,

though no one would have enjoyed
Shaw's criticisms or Lawrence's virility
more than Franklin. He confessed with
gusto that he practised the frugality he
preached just as long as poverty forced
him to—and not a moment longer.

Poor Richard has been regarded by
many as the mentor of early American
capitalism. His advice is certainly keyed
to the two notes: work hard and count
your pennies: the sleeping Fox catches
no poultry; then plough deep, while
Sluggards sleep, and you shall have Corn
to sell and to keep; what maintains one
Vice, would bring up two children;

Many Estates are spent on the Getting
Since Women for Tea forsook Spinning and
    Knitting
And Men for Punch forsook Hewing and
    Splitting.

Not that all *Poor Richard's* moralities
were exhortations to enterprise. Some
were of an earthier sort: a single man is
like the odd half of a pair of scissors; he
that takes a wife takes care; keep your
eyes wide open before marriage, half shut
afterwards; you cannot pluck roses without fear of thorns, nor enjoy a fair wife
without danger of horns. But in nothing
is Franklin more typical of his century
and of his country than in his insistence
that self-reliance and hard work are basic
to liberty. He believed in free speech,
free goods and free men. He opposed
the efforts of all exploiters, whether
merchants in England, Scotch factors in
America, landowners or priests, to re-
strain man's natural freedoms. And
freedom, he argued, paid. Printers, he
said, in his characteristically deflated
way

are educated in the Belief, that when Men
differ in Opinion, both sides ought equally to
have the advantage of being heard by the
Publick; and that when Truth and Error have

Fair Play, the former is always an overmatch
for the latter: Hence they chearfully serve
all contending Writers that pay them well,
without regarding on which side they are of
the Question in Dispute . . .

Certainly his *Almanac* sold: ten thousand copies a year before long. "I grew
in a little time," he said "expert at selling."
And though he did not mention it, expert
at buying. He set up eighteen paper mills,
purchased rags for them, and took the
paper they made, either using it himself
or selling it to other printing houses.
As Professor Bridenbaugh has shown in
his study of *The Colonial Craftsman*,
"it is extremely doubtful if any Englishman was as large a paper dealer as *Poor
Richard* in these years." And he quickly
realized that one source of the successful
salesmanship was his own reputation.

In order to secure my credit and character
as a tradesman, I took care not only to be in
reality industrious and frugal, but to avoid
all *appearances* of the contrary. I dressed
plain and was seen at no places of idle diversion. I never went out a fishing or shooting;
a book, indeed, sometimes debauched me from
my work, but that was seldom, snug and gave
no scandal. . . . Thus being esteemed an
industrious, thriving young man, and paying
duly for what I bought . . . I went on swimmingly.

If this sounds like the wiliness of Mr.
Pepys in the language of Mr. Pooter, it
could be paralleled by similar, if less
frank, reflections in the Papers of many a
contemporary, George Washington included. In a sense all the Revolutionaries were self-made men, and some of
them in making their reputations made a
Revolution. The Yankee virtues tri-
umphed not at Appomattox but at York-
town.

It is true that there were contemporaries too who were not attracted by
Franklin's sentiments. They never won

much approval in the American South, with its open-handed ways, its code of the gentleman, its aversion from trade; and they were anathema to many in Boston. But to Carlyle, and many since his day, Ben Franklin has become "the Father of all the Yankees." To many even outside the Southern States, Yankee is an opprobrious term, a badge of trade and a badge of infamy, yet it was these Yankee values that were transforming the eighteenth-century world. Both Boston and Virginia, in their different ways, were aristocratic: names and connections counted. Franklin lived by trade, prospered by it and was acclaimed across the world. He was completely and avowedly bourgeois, happy in the company of men, and women too, efficient in keeping a contract, adept at conciliation and in the affairs of towns. Virginian Jefferson was afraid of towns as threats to the rural democracy he worked for; Franklin, though he presented himself to the French as a backwoodsman, was only at ease when he was in them. He transformed Philadelphia. To him it owed the fact that it had a city police, the paved and lighted streets that were the surprise of Virginians and New Englanders. To him, too, it owed the American Philosophical Society and the University of Pennsylvania and the first circulating library in America. To him the country — before it had yet been born — owed the efficiency of its postal service, and its first project of a Federation. His Junto might be called the first collection of Rotarians in history, "seeking the promotion of our interests in business by more extensive recommendation." Versatile, businesslike, complaisant by disposition, Franklin strikes a modern note, the first of the joiners and boosters and glad-handers. Well might William Green call him the Patron Saint of Labour, in his practise and preaching of diligence, thrift, caution, his

faith that good causes could be linked to self-advancement, that sweet reasonableness did not prevent a good conceit of oneself. But this doctrine too is out of favour. Hard work and thrift are no longer held to be unquestioned guarantees of success either in Britain or in America. As the *New York Times* put it as long ago as 1938, "*Poor Richard* appeals now only to vulgar minds. . . . Why count pennies when millions of dollars are pouring out from the inexhaustible Federal Horn of Plenty?" It was easier in Franklin's day than in Franklin Roosevelt's to make a case for his Industrious Apprentice.

History, then, has not been very sympathetic to his reputation or to his doctrine. Nor has it dealt very kindly with his political services to the American Revolution. It has become very clear that in his days as a Colonial Agent in London he was working not for the independence of the colonies but for a form of Federal Union. He disapproved of the Boston Tea Party and, until his return to America in 1775, his journalism was much less influential than that of Sam Adams. He admired England, he enjoyed London society, he deprecated violence. And even his services in France are open to question. If one argues that the French Alliance was vital to American success in the Revolution, one must admit Franklin's services: yet French troops, money, arms and commerical privileges were coming through, thanks to Beaumarchais, in secret but abundantly, long before the treaty was signed. It was perhaps the quick loss of New York which checked French intervention as early as 1776. The signing of the Alliance after Saratoga suggests that Vergennes was influenced less by emissaries in Paris than by events in America. And the picture, also, of the homespun patriot at the bar of the Commons in 1765, and that of the fur-capped philosopher at Versailles, the toast of French society, is one that makes little appeal to an age suspicious of histrionics.

Yet this is to deny his diplomatic services—and they were not confined to his years abroad. If as a Colonial Agent he worked for compromise, he worked for it all his life. Standing at the bar of the House, he told the Commons in 1765 that "every assembly on the American continent, and every member in every assembly" had denied Parliament's authority to pass the Stamp Act. As Deputy Postmaster-General of North America he was himself an example of emerging colonial unity. As plain Ben Franklin, large, broad-shouldered, with his big head and square deft hands, self-taught and practical, he was the embodiment of the colonial protest, "the ultimate Whig." In France from 1776 these qualities were held in still higher regard: to Vergennes he was an instrument of French imperial revenge on Britain, to the Encyclopaedists and Physiocrats a natural man from a republican wilderness, to blue stockings a rustic philosopher with civilized tastes, with an approving eye for the ladies and a neat democratic wit. In Paris and in Passy, he was surrounded by an admiring court. His French, no more than passable, seemed charming. His portrait appeared on medallions, rings and snuff boxes. To all Franklin was a proof of republican simplicity and virtue; he was the American, this new man. The fur cap was worn to hide his eczema; it was mistaken for a badge of the frontier. Since he was cast in the rôle of wise and simple philosopher he played the part. He could be Solon and Silenus, gallant and Gallic, to suit all tastes, and not least his own.

In his years in France he showed an uncanny diplomatic skill. He used the same facility in his last great work at the Federal Convention in 1787. In his *Autobiography* he has left a description of diplomatic technique around the Conference table from which we can still learn:—

> I made it a rule to forbear all direct contradiction to the sentiments of others and all positive assertion of my own. I even forbade myself . . . the use of every word or expression in the language that imported a fixed opinion such as "certainly," "undoubtedly," etc.; and I adopted instead of them "I conceive," "I apprehend" or "I imagine" a thing to be so or so, or "It so appears to me at present." When another asserted something that I thought an error, I denied myself the pleasure of contradicting him abruptly and of showing immediately some absurdity in his proposition; and in answering I began by observing that in certain cases or circumstances his opinion would be right, but that in the present case there "appeared" or "seemed to me" some difference, etc. I soon found the advantage of this change . . .

And if he fought for colonial rights and understanding in London in 1765, he was still fighting for tolerance and the other point of view in 1787. The speech that James Wilson delivered for him on the last day of the Convention—he was too old and too infirm to stand—was the product of long experience and expressed that reasonableness that the twentieth century as well as the eighteenth might regard as the closest approximation that finite man can make to wisdom. He appealed to his colleagues among the Founding Fathers who opposed the Constitution to doubt with himself a little of their own infallibility. I confess, he said, that

> I do not entirely approve of this Constitution at present, but Sir, I am not sure I shall never approve it: For having lived long, I have experienced many instances of being obliged, by better information or fuller consideration to change opinion even on important subjects, which I once thought right, but found to be

otherwise. It is therefore that the older I grow the more apt I am to doubt my own judgment, and to pay more respect to the judgment of others . . . I consent, Sir, to this Constitution, because I expect no better, and because I am not sure that it is not the best. The opinions I have had of its errors I sacrifice to the public good. I have never whisper'd a syllable of them abroad. Within these walls they were born, and here they shall die.

One can understand the doubts that have over the last century attached to Franklin's reputation, both personal and political. He was not, like Washington or Jefferson, a Virginian landowner devoting himself to public affairs, and he has been harder to fit into a nationalist mythology. When in 1788 he drew up his will, he began "I, Benjamin Franklin, of Philadelphia, printer, late Minister Plenipotentiary from the United States of America to the Court of France, now President of the State of Pennsylvania." There is a ring of triumph about it, but it is a bourgeois triumph, the success is not sublime but smug. And the sentiments would be repeated, indeed from 1828 would become part of the American political creed. In 1840:

> Old Tip he wears a homespun coat
> He has no ruffled shirt, wirt, wirt,
> If Mat has all the golden plate
> He is a little squirt, wirt, wirt.

In 1861 "From log cabin to White House," in 1940, "I came up the hard way." Dixon Wecter once likened Franklin to a Sancho Panza, "rejoicing in homely wisdom, thinking of belly and pocket-book as he ambles by the side of the greater idealist, the godlike Washington." The fact was that Franklin was infinitely more symbolic, infinitely more dangerous, infinitely more modern-minded, than Washington. And in the contemporary assessments of him there is not a little fear. He was so

adept, riches seemed to come his way so smoothly, he left his grandson a fortune of five hundred thousand dollars, he won the plaudits of foreigners. John Adams, always jealous of the affection of the French for Franklin, seemed to think he had caused the French Revolution. "The best talents in France were blind disciples of Franklin and Turgot, and led the blind to destruction."

Of the fathers of his country, whatever the years might have done to his reputation, Franklin is perhaps the most significant, the most cosmopolitan, the most prescient for the future, the new man. The printer had made himself the first specimen Yankee. He was a successful tradesman in an age of reason, his *Autobiography* is the first American self-revelation of a self-made man. By his *Almanac* and by his career he preached the American faith: reliance on oneself and on one's own efforts, prudence, good sense and the respect of one's neighbours. Like Jefferson he saw no limits to the capacity of free men, as citizens, as workers or as liberal enquirers after truth in many fields. Like Jefferson again, he was a deist. During his years in England, he undertook along with Sir Francis Dashwood a revision of the Prayer Book, and of the Catechism he retained only two questions: "What is your duty to God?" and "What is your duty to your neighbour?" Franklin's faith in political freedom was linked to a faith in economic freedom, and to a faith in scientific freedom, too. He ranged widely and he ranged easily: there is no sense of superiority, rather the reverse, but there is certainly an effortlessness that comes not from Balliol or Boston but from a confidence in the capacity of what he called "the middling people." Franklin learnt by reading and by observation, and what he learnt he sought to apply. The test was empirical, and the tests were

endless. Human, gregarious, wordly, en-
quiring yet unspeculative, restless yet
equable in temper, unpompous, a preacher
of moralities who honoured them as much
in the breach as in the observance, a coun-
sellor of prudence who was always ready
to take a chance, a plain man who liked
the graces and the comforts of life, a master of slogans who never deceived himself
by them, sceptic and idealist and a lover of
children, he has left his mark conspicu-
ously on the American character. He was
father of all the Yankees, perhaps—for
did not *Poor Richard* say "The cat in
gloves catches no mice?"—but ambassador
also to two great kingdoms. His wordly
wisdom was suited to the *philosophes* in
Paris and in Edinburgh; it was suited, too,
to the old wives in the chimney corner,
summing up a lifetime of neighbourly
experience. He was at home in France. In
England, he said, he was thought of as too
much of an American, and in America
was deemed too much an Englishman. He
was rightly thought of as a citizen of the
world, and this, too, is part of his legacy
to Americans. He wrote his own epitaph,
perhaps the most famous of all American
epitaphs: "The Body of B. Franklin,
Printer, (Like the Cover of an old Book,
Its Contents torn out and Stript of its
Lettering and Gilding) Lies here, food for
Worms. But the Work shall not be lost;
For it will (as he believ'd), appear once
more, in a new and more elegant Edition,
Revised and Corrected, by the Author."

JOHN WILLIAM WARD (b. 1922), professor of history at Amherst College, discusses the many masks of the Franklin image in the *Autobiography*. Franklin deliberately played the role that the situation seemed to demand. The *Autobiography*, Ward maintains, is not about success itself; it is about the character building that makes success possible. Franklin's swift rise to prominence, together with his social mobility and adaptability, raises the question of identity, a typically American question: "Who am I?"*

John William Ward

Franklin: His Masks and His Character

Benjamin Franklin bulks large in our national consciousness, sharing room with Washington and Jefferson and Lincoln. Yet it is hard to say precisely what it means to name Franklin one of our cultural heroes. He was, as one book about him has it, "many-sided." The sheer variety of his character has made it possible to praise him and damn him with equal vigor. At home, such dissimilar Yankees as the laconic Calvin Coolidge and the passionate Theodore Parker could each find reason to admire him. Abroad, David Hume could say that he was "the first great man of letters" for whom Europe was "beholden" to America. Yet D. H. Lawrence, brought up, he tells us, in the industrial wastelands of midland England on the pious saws of "Poor Richard," could only "utter a long, loud curse" against "this dry, moral utilitarian little democrat."

Part of the difficulty in comprehending Franklin's meaning is due to the opposites he seems to have contained with complete serenity within his own personality. He was an eminently reasonable man who maintained a deep skepticism about the power of reason. He was a model of industriousness who, preaching the gospel of hard work, kept his shop only until it kept him and retired at forty-two. He was a cautious and prudent man who was a revolutionist. And, to name only one more seeming contradiction, he was one who had a keen eye

---

*From John William Ward, "Who Was Benjamin Franklin?" in *The American Scholar,* Vol. 32 (Autumn, 1963), pp. 541–553. Footnotes deleted.

103

for his own advantage and personal advancement who spent nearly all his adult life in the service of others. Small wonder that there have been various interpretations of so various a character.

The problem may seem no problem at all. Today, when we all know that the position of the observer determines the shape of reality, we observe the observer. If Franklin, seeing to it that the streets of Philadelphia are well lit and swept clean at a moderate price, that no fires rage, does not appeal to D. H. Lawrence, we tend not to think of Franklin. We think of Lawrence; we remember his atavistic urge to explore the dark and passionate underside of life and move on. Franklin contained in his own character so many divergent aspects that each observer can make the mistake of seeing one aspect as all and celebrate or despise Franklin accordingly. Mr. I. Bernard Cohen, who has written so well on so much of Franklin, has remarked that "an account of Franklin . . . is apt to be a personal testament of the commentator concerning the America he most admires." Or condemns.

Yet there still remains the obstinate fact that Franklin could mean so many things to so many men, that he was so many-sided, that he did contain opposites, that he was, in other words, so many different characters. One suspects that here is the single most important thing about Franklin. Rather than spend our energies trying to find some consistency in this protean, many-sided figure, trying to resolve who Franklin truly was, we might perhaps better accept his variety itself as our major problem and try to understand that. To insist on the importance of the question, "Who was Benjamin Franklin?" may finally be more conclusive than to agree upon an answer.

The place to begin to ask the question is with the *Memoirs,* with the *Autobiography* as we have come to call them, and the place to begin there is with the history of the text. Fascinating in and of itself, the history of the text gives us an initial lead into the question of the elusiveness of Franklin's personality.

The *Autobiography* was written in four parts. The first part, addressed by Franklin to his son, William, was begun during some few weeks in July and August, 1771, while Franklin was visiting with his friend, Jonathan Shipley, the Bishop of St. Asaph, in Hampshire, England. Franklin was then sixty-five years old. As he wrote the first part he also carefully made a list of topics he would subsequently treat. Somehow the manuscript and list fell into the hands of one Abel James who eleven years later wrote Franklin, returning to him the list of topics but not the first part of the manuscript, urging him to take up his story once again. This was in 1782, or possibly early in January, 1783. Franklin was in France as one of the peace commissioners. He wrote the second part in France in 1784, after the achievement of peace, indicating the beginning and the ending of this short second part in the manuscript itself.

In 1785, Franklin returned to America, promising to work on the manuscript during the voyage. Instead he wrote three of his utilitarian essays: on navigation, on how to avoid smoky streetlamp chimneys, and on his famous stove. He did not return to his life's story until 1788. Then, after retiring from the presidency of the state of Pennsylvania in the spring, Franklin, quite sick, made his will and put his house in order before turning again to his own history. This was in August, 1788. Franklin was eighty-three years old, in pain, and preparing for death. The third part is the longest part of the autobiography, less interesting than the first two, and for many years was thought to conclude the manuscript.

In 1789, Franklin had his grandson, Benjamin Franklin Bache, make two fair copies of Parts I, II and III in order to send them to friends abroad, Benjamin Vaughan in England and M. le Veillard in France. Then, sometime before his death in April, 1790, Franklin added the last and fourth part, some seven and one-half manuscript pages, which was not included, naturally, in the fair copies sent abroad. For the rest, Mr. Max Farrand, our authority on the history of the text:

After [Franklin's] death, the publication of the autobiography was eagerly awaited, as its existence was widely known, but for nearly thirty years the reading public had to content itself with French translations of the first and second parts, which were again translated from the French into other languages, and even retranslated into English. When the authorized English publication finally appeared in 1818, it was not taken from the original manuscript but from a copy, as was the preceding French version of the first part. The copy, furthermore, did not include the fourth and last part, which also reached the public in a French translation in 1828.

... the complete autobiography was not printed in English from the original manuscript until 1868, nearly eighty years after Franklin's death.

The story is, as I have said, interesting in and of itself. The tangled history of one of our most important texts has its own fascination, but it also provides us the first clue to our question. Surely it must strike any reader of the *Autobiography* as curious that a character who speaks so openly should at the same time seem so difficult to define. But the history of the text points the way to an answer.

All we need do is ask why Franklin wrote his memoirs.

When the Quaker, Abel James, wrote Franklin, returning his list of topics and asking "kind, humane, and benevolent Ben Franklin" to continue his life's story, "a work which would be useful and entertaining not only to a few but to millions," Franklin sent the letter on to his friend, Benjamin Vaughan, asking for advice. Vaughan concurred. He too urged Franklin to publish the history of his life because he could think of no "more efficacious advertisement" of America than Franklin's history. "All that has happened to you," he reminded Franklin, "is also connected with the detail of the manners and situation of a rising people." Franklin included James's and Vaughan's letters in his manuscript to explain why he resumed his story. What had gone before had been written for his family; "what follows," he said in his "Memo," "was written . . . in compliance with the advice contained in these letters, and accordingly intended for the public. The affairs of the Revolution occasioned the interruption."

The point is obvious enough. When Franklin resumed his story, he did so in full self-consciousness that he was offering himself to the world as a representative type, the American. Intended for the public now, his story was to be an example for young Americans, as Abel James would have it, and an advertisement to the world, as Benjamin Vaughan would have it. We had just concluded a successful revolution; the eyes of all the world were upon us. Just as America had succeeded in creating itself a nation, Franklin set out to show how the American went about creating his own character. As Benjamin Vaughan said, Franklin's life would "give a noble rule and example of self-education" because of Franklin's "discovery that the thing is in many a man's private power." So what follows is no longer the simple annals of Franklin's life for the benefit of his son. Benjamin Franklin plays his proper role. He becomes "The American."

How well he filled the part that his public urged him to play, we can see by observing what he immediately proceeds to provide. In the pages that follow James's and Vaughan's letters, Franklin quickly treats four matters: the establishment of a lending library, that is, the means for satisfying the need for self-education; the importance of frugality and industriousness in one's calling; the social utility of religion; and, of course, the thirteen rules for ordering one's life. Here, in a neat package, were all the materials that went into the making of the self-made man. This is how one goes about making a success of one's self. If the sentiments of our Declaration were to provide prompt notes for European revolutions, then Franklin, as the American Democrat, acted them out. Family, class, religious orthodoxy, higher education: all these were secondary to character and common sense. The thing was in many a man's private power.

If we look back now at the first part, the opening section addressed by Franklin to his son, William, we can see a difference and a similarity. The difference is, of course, in the easy and personal tone, the more familiar manner, appropriate to a communication with one's son. It is in these early pages that Franklin talks more openly about his many *errata,* his "frequent intrigues with low women," and displays that rather cool and calculating attitude toward his wife. Rather plain dealing, one might think, at least one who did not know that William was a bastard son.

But the similarity between the two

parts is more important. The message is the same, although addressed to a son, rather than to the world: how to go about making a success. "From the poverty and obscurity in which I was born and in which I passed my earliest years," writes the father to the son, "I have raised myself to a state of affluence and some degree of celebrity in the world." A son, especially, must have found that "some" hard to take. But the career is not simply anecdotal: "my posterity will perhaps be desirous of learning the means, which I employed, and which, thanks to Providence, so well succeeded with me. They may also deem them fit to be imitated." The story is exemplary, although how the example was to affect a son who was, in 1771, about forty years old and already Royal Governor of New Jersey is another matter.

The story has remained exemplary because it is the success story to beat all success stories: the runaway apprentice printer who rose to dine with kings; the penniless boy, walking down Market Street with two large rolls under his arms, who was to sit in Independence Hall and help create a new nation. But notice that the story does not deal with the success itself. That is presumed, of course, but the *Autobiography* never gets to the later and more important years because the *Autobiography* is not about success. It is about the formation of the character that makes success possible. The subject of the *Autobiography* is the making of a character. Having lifted himself by his own bootstraps, Franklin described it that way: "I have raised myself." We were not to find the pat phrase until the early nineteenth century when the age of the common man made the style more common: "the self-made man." The character was for life, of course, and not for fiction where we usually expect to encounter the made-up, but that should not prevent us from looking a little more closely at the act of creation. We can look in two ways: first, by standing outside the *Autobiography* and assessing it by what we know from elsewhere; second, by reading the *Autobiography* itself more closely.

A good place to begin is with those years in France around the end of the Revolution. It is so delicious an episode in plain Ben's life. More importantly —as Franklin said, one can always find a principle to justify one's inclinations— it is in these very years at Passy that Franklin, in response to James's and Vaughan's letters, wrote those self-conscious pages of the second part of the *Autobiography*. Just as he wrote the lines, he played them. As Carl Van Doren has written, "the French were looking for a hero who should combine the reason and wit of Voltaire with the primitive virtues celebrated by Rousseau. . . . [Franklin] denied them nothing." This is the period of the simple Quaker dress, the fur cap and the spectacles. France went wild in its adulation and Franklin knew why. "Think how this must appear," he wrote a friend, "among the powdered heads of Paris."

But he was also moving with equal ease in that world, the world of the powdered heads of Paris, one of the most cosmopolitan, most preciously civilized societies in history. Although he was no Quaker, Franklin was willing to allow the French to think so. They called him *"le bon Quackeur."* The irony was unintentional, a matter of translation. But at the same time that he was filling the role of the simple backwoods democrat, the innocent abroad, he was also playing cavalier in the brilliant salon of Madame Helvétius, the widow of the French philosopher. Madame Helvétius is supposed

to have been so beautiful that Fontenelle, the great popularizer of Newton, who lived to be one hundred years old, was said to have paid her the most famous compliment of the age: "Ah, madame, if I were only eighty again!" Madame Helvétius was sixty when Franklin knew her and the classic anecdote of their acquaintance is that Madame Helvétius is said to have reproached him for not coming to see her, for putting off his long anticipated visit. Franklin replied, "Madame, I am waiting until the nights are longer." There was also Madame Brillon, not a widow, who once wrote to Franklin, "People have the audacity to criticize my pleasant habit of sitting on your knee, and yours of always asking me for what I always refuse."

Some, discovering this side of Franklin, have written him off simply as a rather lively old lecher. Abigail Adams, good New England lady that she was, was thoroughly shocked. She set Madame Helvétius down as a "very bad woman." But Franklin, despite his public style, was not so provincial. He appealed to Madame Brillon that he had spent so many days with her that surely she could spend one night with him. She mockingly called him a sophist. He then appealed to her charity and argued that it was in the design of Providence that she grant him his wish. If somehow a son of the Puritans, Franklin had grown far beyond the reach of their sermonizing. Thomas Hooker had thought, "It's a grievous thing to the loose person, he cannot have his pleasures but he must have his guilt and gall with them." But Franklin wrote Madame Brillon, "Reflect how many of our duties [Providence] has ordained naturally to be pleasures; and that it has had the goodness besides, to give the name of sin to several of them so that we might enjoy them the more."

All this is delightful enough, and for more one need only turn to Carl Van Doren's biography from which I have taken these anecdotes, but what it points to is as important as it is entertaining. It points to Franklin's great capacity to respond to the situation in which he found himself and to play the expected role, to prepare a face to meet the faces that he met. He could, in turn, be the homespun, rustic philosopher or the mocking cavalier, the witty sophist. He knew what was expected of him.

The discovery should not surprise any reader of the *Autobiography*. Throughout it, Franklin insists always on the distinction between appearance and reality, between what he is and what he seems to be.

In order to secure my credit and character as a tradesman, I took care not only to be in *reality* industrious and frugal, but to avoid all *appearances* of the contrary. I dressed plain and was seen at no places of idle diversion. I never went out a fishing or shooting; a book, indeed, sometimes debauched me from my work, but that was seldom, snug, and gave no scandal; and to show that I was not above my business, I sometimes brought home the paper I purchased at the stores, thro' the streets on a wheelbarrow. Thus being esteemed an industrious, thriving young man, and paying duly for what I bought, the merchants who imported stationery solicited my custom; others proposed supplying me with books, and I went on swimmingly.

Now, with this famous passage, one must be careful. However industrious and frugal Franklin may in fact have been, he knew that for the business of social success virtue counts for nothing without its public dress. In Franklin's world there has to be someone in the woods to hear the tree fall. Private virtue might bring one to stand before the King of kings, but if one wants to sit down and sup with the kings of this world, then one must help them see one's merit. There are always in this world, as Franklin pointed out, "a number of rich merchants, nobility, states, and princes who have need of honest instruments for the management of their affairs, and such being so rare [I] have endeavoured to convince young persons, that no qualities are so likely to make a poor man's fortune as those of probity and integrity."

Yet if one wants to secure one's credit in the world by means of one's character, then the character must be of a piece. There can be no false gesture; the part must be played well. When Franklin drew up his list of virtues they contained, he tells us, only twelve. But a Quaker friend "kindly" informed him that he was generally thought proud and overbearing and rather insolent; he proved it by examples. So Franklin added humility to his list; but, having risen in the world and content with the degree of celebrity he had achieved, he could not bring himself to be humble. "I cannot boast of much success in acquiring the *reality* of this virtue, but I had a good deal with regard to the *appearance* of it."

He repeats, at this point, what he had already written in the first part of his story. He forswears all "positive assertion." He drops from his vocabulary such words as "certainly" and "undoubtedly" and adopts a tentative manner. He remembers how he learned to speak softly, to put forward his opinions, not dogmatically, but by saying, "'I imagine' a thing to be so or so, or 'It so appears to me at present.'" As he had put it to his son earlier, he discovered the Socratic method, "was charmed with it, adopted it, dropped my abrupt contradiction and positive argumentation, and put on the humble enquirer." For good reason:

"this habit . . . has been of great advantage to me."

What saves all this in the *Autobiography* from being merely repellent is Franklin's self-awareness, his good humor in telling us about the part he is playing, the public clothes he is putting on to hide what his public will not openly buy. "In reality," he writes, drawing again the distinction from appearance, "there is perhaps no one of our natural passions so hard to subdue as *pride;* disguise it, struggle with it, beat it down, stifle it, mortify it as much as one pleases, it is still alive and will every now and then peep out and show itself. You will see it perhaps often in this history. For even if I could conceive that I had completely overcome it, I should probably be proud of my humility." Here, despite the difference in tone, Franklin speaks like that other and contrasting son of the Puritans, Jonathan Edwards, on the nature of true virtue. Man, if he could achieve virtue, would inevitably be proud of the achievement and so, at the moment of success, fall back into sin.

The difference is, of course, in the tone. The insight is the same but Franklin's skeptical and untroubled self-acceptance is far removed from Edwards' troubled and searching self-doubt. Franklin enjoys the game. Mocking himself, he quietly lures us, in his Yankee deadpan manner, with the very bait he has just described. After having told us that he early learned to "put on the humble enquirer" and to affect a self-depreciating pose, he quotes in his support the line from Alexander Pope, "To speak, though sure, with seeming diffidence." Pope, Franklin immediately goes on to say, "might have joined with this line that which he has coupled with another, I think less properly, 'For want of modesty is want of sense.'"

If you ask why *less properly,* I must repeat the lines,

> Immodest words admit of *no defence,*
> For want of modesty is want of sense.

Now is not the "want of sense" (where a man is so unfortunate as to want it) some apology for his "want of modesty"? and would not the lines stand more justly thus?

> Immodest words admit *but* this defense
> That want of modesty is want of sense.

This, however, I should submit to better judgements.

Having been so bold as to correct a couplet of the literary giant of the age, Franklin quietly retreats and defers to the judgment of those better able to say than he. Having just described the humble part he has decided to play, he immediately acts it out. If we get the point, we chuckle with him; if we miss the point, that only proves its worth.

But one of the functions of laughter is to dispel uneasiness and in Franklin's case the joke is not enough. Our uneasiness comes back when we stop to remember that he is, as his friends asked him to, writing his story as an efficacious advertisement. We must always ask whether Franklin's disarming candor in recounting how things went on so swimmingly may not be yet another role, still another part he is playing. Actually, even with Yale's sumptuous edition of Franklin's papers, we know little about Franklin's personal life in the early years, except through his own account. The little we do know suggests that his way to wealth and success was not the smooth and open path he would have us believe. This leads us, then, if we cannot answer finally the question who Franklin was, to a different question. What does it mean to say that a character so changeable, so elusive, somehow represents American culture? What is there in Franklin's style that makes him, as we say, characteristic?

At the outset in colonial America, with men like John Winthrop, there was always the assumption that one would be called to one's appropriate station in life and labor in it for one's own good and the good of society. Magistrates would be magistrates and printers would be printers. But in the world in which Franklin moved, the magistrates, like Governor Keith of Pennsylvania who sends Franklin off on a wild-goose chase to England, prove to be frauds while the plain, leather-aproned set went quietly about the work of making society possible at all, creating the institutions—the militia, the fire companies, the libraries, the hospitals, the public utilities—that made society habitable. The notion that underlay an orderly, hierarchical society failed to make sense of such a world. It proved impossible to keep people in their place.

One need only consider in retrospect how swiftly Franklin moved upward through the various levels of society to see the openness, the fluidity of his world. Simply because he is a young man with some books, Governor Burnet of New York asks to see him. While in New Jersey on a job printing money he meets and makes friends with all the leaders of that provincial society. In England, at the coffeehouses, he chats with Mandeville and meets the great Dr. Henry Pemberton who was seeing the third edition of Newton's *Principia* through the press. As Franklin said, diligent in his calling, he raised himself by some degree.

The Protestant doctrine of calling, of industriousness in the world, contained dynamite for the orderly, hierarchical, social structure it was originally meant to support. The unintended consequence showed itself within two generations. Those who were abstemious, frugal and hardworking made a success in the world. They rose. And society, rather than the static and closed order in which, in Winthrop's words, "some must be rich some poor, some high and eminent in power and dignitie; others meane and in subieccion," turned out to be dynamic, fluid and open.

If there is much of our national character implicit in Franklin's career, it is because, early in our history, he represents a response to the rapid social change that has remained about the only constant in American society. He was the self-made man, the jack-of-all-trades. He taught thirteen rules to sure success and purveyed do-it-yourself kits for those who, like himself, constituted a "rising" people. Franklin stands most clearly as an exemplary American because his life's story is a witness to the uncertainties about social status that have characterized our society, a society caught up in the constant process of change. The question, "Who was Benjamin Franklin?" is a critical question to ask of Franklin because it is the question to which Franklin himself is constantly seeking an answer. In a society in which there are no outward, easily discernible marks of social status, the question always is, as we put it in the title of reference works that are supposed to provide the answer, "Who's Who?"

Along with the uncertainties generated by rapid social mobility, there is another aspect to the difficulty we have in placing Franklin, an aspect that is more complex and harder to state, but just as important and equally characteristic. It takes us back again to the Puritans. In Puritan religious thought there was originally a dynamic equipoise between two opposite thrusts, the tension between an inward, mystical, personal experience of God's grace and the demands for an outward, sober, socially responsible ethic, the tension between faith and works, between the essence of religion and its outward show. Tremendous energy went into sustaining these polarities in the early years but, as the original piety waned, itself undermined by the worldly success that benefited from the doctrine of calling, the synthesis split in two and resulted in the eighteenth century in Jonathan Edwards and Benjamin Franklin, similar in so many ways, yet so radically unlike.

Franklin, making his own world as he makes his way through it, pragmatically rejects the old conundrum whether man does good works because he is saved, or is saved because he does good works. "Vicious actions are not hurtful because they are forbidden, but forbidden because they are hurtful," he decides, and then in an added phrase calmly throws out the God-centered universe of his forebears, "the nature of man alone considered."

Content with his success, blandly sure it must be in the design of Providence that printers hobnob with kings, Franklin simply passes by the problem of the relation between reality and appearance. In this world, appearance is sufficient. Humanely skeptical that the essence can ever be caught, Franklin decided to leave the question to be answered in the next world, if there proved to be one. For this world, a "tolerable character" was enough and he "valued it properly." The result was a commonsense utilitarianism which sometimes verges toward sheer crassness. But it worked. For this world, what others think of you is what is important. If Franklin, viewed from the perspective of Max Weber and students of the Protestant ethic, can seem to be the representative, *par excellence,*

of the character who internalizes the imperatives of his society and steers his own course unaided through the world, from a slightly different perspective he also turns out to be the other-directed character David Riesman has described, constantly attuned to the expectations of those around him, responding swiftly to the changing situations that demand he play different roles.

We admire, I think, the lusty good sense of the man who triumphs in the world that he accepts, yet at the same time we are uneasy with the man who wears so many masks that we are never sure who is there behind them. Yet it is this, this very difficulty of deciding whether we admire Franklin or suspect him, that makes his character an archetype for our national experience. There are great advantages to be had in belonging to a culture without clearly defined classes, without an establishment, but there is, along with the advantages, a certain strain, a necessary uneasiness. In an open and pluralistic society we have difficulty "placing" people, as we say. Think how often in our kind of society when we meet someone for the first time how our second or third question is apt to be, "What do you do?" Never, "Who are you?" The social role is enough, but in our more reflective moments we realize not so, and in our most reflective moments we realize it will never do for our own selves. We may be able to, but we do not want to go through life as a doctor, lawyer or Indian chief. We want to be ourselves, as we say. And at the beginning of our national experience, Benjamin Franklin not only puts the question that still troubles us in our kind of society, "Who's Who?" He also raises the question that lies at the heart of the trouble: "Who am I?"

Suggestions for Further Reading

Benjamin Franklin has been the subject of many biographies, four of which have survived searching scholarly scrutiny as well as the probes of literary critics. Carl Van Doren's excellent biography, *Benjamin Franklin* (New York, 1938), shows Franklin as a many-sided man who loved life and enjoyed sensuous pleasures. Carl L. Becker's superb sketch of Franklin in the *Dictionary of American Biography*, V (New York, 1946), 585–598, stresses Franklin's concern with self-improvement and his sly sense of humor. Verner W. Crane, in *Benjamin Franklin and a Rising People* (Boston, 1954), portrays Franklin as one of the most influential figures in the early American period. Supplementing these three studies is Alfred Owen Aldridge, *Benjamin Franklin, Philosopher and Man* (Philadelphia, 1965), a recent biography with new material on the roguish side of Franklin's character. In a later study, *Benjamin Franklin and Nature's God* (Durham, N.C., 1967), Aldridge analyzes Franklin's lifelong search for spiritual satisfaction.

Among the older biographies of Franklin still worth reading are John B. McMaster, *Benjamin Franklin as a Man of Letters* (Boston, 1887) and Paul Leicester Ford, *The Many-Sided Franklin* (New York, 1889). James Parton, *Life and Times of Benjamin Franklin*, 2 vols. (New York, 1864) contains errors but continues to be the most comprehensive of all the Franklin biographies.

A number of older biographical studies by foreign writers have also helped to illuminate the character and accomplishments of Franklin. Among these are Phillips Russell, *Benjamin Franklin, the First Civilized American* (London, 1927), emphasizing Franklin's experiences abroad, and Bernard Fay, *Franklin the Apostle of Modern Times* (London, 1929), which gives an admiring European view of Franklin.

During recent decades a number of books and articles have dealt with special aspects of Franklin's achievement. The Franklin Institute, *Meet Dr. Franklin* (Philadelphia, 1943) is a collection of papers delivered at a symposium. It includes: Carl Van Doren, "Meet Dr. Franklin"; Max Farrand, "Self-Portraiture: the *Autobiography*"; Bernhard Knollenberg, "Benjamin Franklin: Philosophical Revolutionist"; Lawrence C. Wroth, "Benjamin Franklin: The Printer at Work"; and Julian P. Boyd, "Dr. Franklin: Friend of the Indians." Gerald Stourzh, *Benjamin Franklin and American Foreign Policy* (Chicago, 1954) is a stimulating work appraising Franklin's career as a diplomat. Franklin's life as an overseas agent is gracefully sketched in Roger Burlingame, *Benjamin Franklin, Envoy Extraordinary* (New York, 1967). I. Bernard Cohen, *Franklin and Newton, An Inquiry into Speculative Newtonian Experimental Science and Franklin's Work in Electricity as an Example Thereof* (Philadelphia, 1956) is a major work on Franklin's achievements as an experimental scientist. Paul W. Connor, *Poor Richard's Politics, Benjamin Franklin and the New American Order* (New York, 1965) argues that Franklin's writings exhibit a coherent political theory reflecting the beginnings of American nationalism. Thomas Fleming, *The Man Who Dared Lightning: A New Look at Benjamin Franklin* (New York, 1971) portrays Franklin as a great leader who presided over the birth of the American nation. Two additional (but contrasting) studies on Franklin's politics are William S. Hanna, *Benjamin Franklin and Pennsylvania Politics* (Stanford, Calif., 1964) and James H. Hutson, "Benjamin Franklin and Pennsylvania Politics, 1751–

1755: A Reappraisal," *Pennsylvania Magazine of History and Biography,* XCIII (July, 1969), 303–371. Two significant studies analyzing Franklin imagery are Richard Miles, "The American Image of Benjamin Franklin," *American Quarterly,* IX (Summer, 1957), 117–143, and Douglass Adair's brilliant "Fame and the Founding Fathers," in Edmund P. Willis, ed., *Fame and the Founding Fathers* (Bethlehem, Pa., 1966), 27–61. Glen Weaver, "Benjamin Franklin and the Pennsylvania Germans," *William and Mary Quarterly,* XIV (October, 1957), 536–539, examines Franklin's relations with an important minority group. Claude-Anne Lopez, *Mon Cher Papa: Franklin and the Ladies of Paris* (New Haven, 1966) is a well-written, amusing narrative of Franklin's social activities in France, and Max Hall, *Benjamin Franklin and Polly Baker, The History of a Literary Deception* (Chapel Hill, N.C., 1960) is a convincing investigation of the history of one of Franklin's "tall stories." Antonio Pace, *Benjamin Franklin in Italy* (Philadelphia, 1958) emphasizes Franklin's fascination with Italian culture. A critical appraisal of Franklin as a thinker and philosopher is made by Ralph L. Ketcham in *Benjamin Franklin* (New York, 1965), and John Hardin Best praises Franklin's theories on the functions of schools and colleges in *Benjamin Franklin on Education* (New York, 1962).

The best book-length study of Franklin as a writer is Bruce Ingham Granger, *Benjamin Franklin, An American Man of Letters* (Ithaca, N.Y., 1964). A perceptive summary of Franklin's literary interests is in a pamphlet, *Benjamin Franklin* (Minneapolis, 1962) by Theodore Hornberger. An issue of *The Journal of Library History,* II (October, 1967), 267–334, is devoted to Margaret Barton Korty's carefully documented study, "Franklin's World of Books." This is an outgrowth of her earlier study, *Benjamin Franklin and Eighteenth Century Libraries* (Philadelphia, 1965).

Two additional books on Franklin should be mentioned. A definitive investigation of the numerous portraits of Franklin is in Charles Coleman Sellers, *Benjamin Franklin in Portraiture* (New Haven, 1962). The general reader will value the varied collection of Franklin's writings brought together in one volume and edited by Carl Van Doren, *Benjamin Franklin's Autobiographical Writings* (New York, 1945).

The collected writings of Franklin are to be found in two reliable editions. Albert Henry Smyth, ed., *The Writings of Benjamin Franklin,* 10 vols. (New York, 1905–1907) unfortunately omits a number of important items written by Franklin as well as letters written by other people to him. The new edition of *The Papers of Benjamin Franklin,* edited by Leonard Labaree *et al.,* 14 vols. to date (New Haven, 1970), is one of the best sources on colonial eighteenth-century society and promises to be the definitive edition of his work. An excellent critique of the editorial work in the Labaree edition is found in J. A. Leo Lemay, "Franklin and the *Autobiography,* An Essay on Recent Scholarship," *Eighteenth-Century Studies,* I (December, 1967), 185–211. Among the criticisms made by Lemay is that the editors do not print or mention all writings attributed to Franklin (*ibid.,* p. 186). The Labaree edition of the *Autobiography of Benjamin Franklin* (New Haven, 1964) supersedes all earlier editions including Max Farrand's single text, conflated version. However, detailed inspection of the original manuscript of Franklin's *Autobiography* at the Huntington Library (and an exact photostat copy) reveals that not all of Franklin's slight revisions are included in the Yale edition by Labaree. Thus, as Lemay points out, Max Farrand's Parallel Text Edition (Berkeley, Calif., 1949) continues to have a superior text (in spite of criticisms by Yale editors, p. 38). Yet the Yale text is accurate, and the editorial commentary and introduction are superb, making it the best overall edition of the *Autobiography* that has been published.

For bibliographical data, the serious student of Franklin should consult the revised edition of *Benjamin Franklin, Representative Selections, with Introduction, Bibliography, and Notes,* edited by Chester E. Jorgenson and Frank Luther Mott, published in paperback in the American Century Series by Hill and Wang (New York, 1962). The selected bibliography in this work, pp. cli–clxxxix, is the best general bibliography on Franklin in print. Useful references are also to be found in Robert E. Spiller *et al.* eds., *Literary History of the United States* (New York, 1948), III, 507–515, and in "Bibliographical Supplement," edited by Richard M. Ludwig, 1959, pp. 123–

126. Paul Leicester Ford, *Franklin Bibliography: A List of Books Written by, or Relating to Benjamin Franklin* (New York, 1889) includes useful materials published before the turn of the century.

BERKSHIRE
STUDIES IN
HISTORY

Robert Allen Skotheim

Totalitarianism and American Social Thought

Berkshire Studies in Minority History

Under the General Editorship of
Moses Rischin, *San Francisco State College*

Professor Rischin, author of *The Promised City*, nominee for the Pulitzer Prize, received his doctorate at Harvard University. He has been a Guggenheim Fellow, an ACLS Fellow, and a Fulbright Lecturer in American History. He has taught at UCLA, Uppsala University, and Brandeis University. He is author of *The American Gospel of Success* and *Our Own Kind.*

CONCENTRATION CAMPS USA: JAPANESE AMERICANS AND WORLD WAR II

by Roger Daniels,
State University of New York at Fredonia

This volume offers the first treatment by a professional historian of the social, political, and military aspects of the Japanese-American evacuation. Using a combination of regional and archival materials, the author analyzes both the persecutors and the victims and relates this special instance of persecution to the entire fabric of American racism. This *Berkshire Study* shows how undemocratic decisions can be made in a democratic society.
September 1971 / 244 pages / $3.50 paper

Berkshire Studies in American History

Under the General Editorship of
Robert E. Burke,
University of Washington
Professor Burke received his Ph.D. at the University of California, Berkeley.

He is managing editor of the *Pacific Northwest Quarterly* and general editor of the *American Library* reprint series (University of Washington Press). He is author of several books, including *Olson's New Deal for California, The American Nation,* Fourth Edition (co-author), *The Federal Union,* Fourth Edition (co-author), and *A History of American Democracy,* Third Edition (co-author).

TOTALITARIANISM AND AMERICAN SOCIAL THOUGHT

by Robert A. Skotheim,
University of Colorado
The broad concern of this book is with the changing climates of opinion in the United States between the early 1900's and the 1970's. The essays included are concerned with certain assumptions, methods, and value judgments in the social thought of some of the intellectuals who expressed characteristics of the changing climates of opinion. The author attempts to indicate the relevance of the idea of totalitarianism, integral to the history of modern American social thought, to these assumptions, methods, and value judgments. A brief bibliographical essay appears at the end of this *Berkshire Study.*
September 1971 / 144 pages / $3.00 paper

Note: The *Berkshire Studies* described above are only two of many volumes to come in each series.

AMERICAN HISTORY: A Problems Approach
In Two Volumes
by Herman L. Crow and William L. Turnbull, both of **Tarrant County Junior College**

This new text-reader takes a "problems approach" to American history. It combines a chronological narrative with essays that contain divergent viewpoints on controversial issues, so that the student can weigh evidence and reach his own conclusions. It is creative history—forcing the reader to doubt, to inquire, and to seek a strategy of logic and coherence for solving historical and contemporary problems. Questions posed in the introduction to each group of essays are open-ended, eliciting maximum thought and relating the past to the present. **Volume I: April 1971/480 pages/$4.75 paper; Volume II: January 1972.**

AMERICA MOVES WEST, FIFTH EDITION

by Robert E. Riegel, *Dartmouth College,* and Robert G. Athearn, *University of Colorado*

The movement of settlers and their first contact with native Indians, and the development of a culture from politics and literature are incisively covered in this updated history of the American frontier until 1900. The authors begin their exposition with the arrival of the first white settlers on the Atlantic coast. Investigation then proceeds into an in-depth treatment of social, economic, and intellectual factors.

1970/651 pages/$11.95 cloth (tent.)

FROM HOLT, RINEHART AND WINSTON, INC.
383 Madison Avenue, New York 10017

TO BE AN INDIAN

Edited by **Herbert T. Hoover** and **Joseph H. Cash,** both of the University of South Dakota

Few of the European and American historians who have written about the American Indian have thought to ask the Indian himself about his past, and even fewer have made any attempt to show the history of these people through their own eyes. In 1967, under the sponsorship of Miss Doris Duke, the American Indian Research Project came into being at the University of South Dakota. **To Be An Indian** is the first publication to document the dramatic results of the Project. This book presents an extraordinarily poignant and revealing account of Indian history and culture—from the mythical to the present — in the words of the Indians themselves.

Over 800 interviews were conducted over a five-year period, and the testimonies collected by Professors Hoover and Cash cover such topics as the origins of the American Indian, the impact of the Indian Reorganization Act of 1934, the significance of the Native American Church, the life-style of an Indian on a reservation fifty years ago, the problems of relocation and industrial employment, the problems of Indian education, and many others. The narrators are articulate, thoughtful, concerned, and informed citizens of the United States, telling it as it is now. These are their words and this is their book. Approximately 84 pages of illustrations.

1972   260 pages $3.95 paper (tent.)

THE INDIAN IN AMERICAN HISTORY

Edited by **Francis Paul Prucha,** Marquette University

This American Problem Study presents fourteen selections by American historians — among them Roy Harvey Pearce, Reginald Horseman, Bernard W. Sheehan, and Vine Deloria — that describe and interpret different aspects of the Indian-white conflict and adjustment from colonial times to the present. The book is divided into four parts: writings which treat dispossession of the Indians; writings which refute criticisms of government action; writings concerned with attempts to assimilate Indians into white culture; and contemporary analyses of the Indians. An annotated bibliography appends the text.

1972   128 pages $2.45 (tent.) paper